ONE HUMAN...BEING

*Observations and Inspirations
from Within the Journey*

DANNY REDDICK

Publisher:
One Human...Being
P.O. Box 2468
Frederiksted, USVI 00841-2468
720-270-4240
Danny Reddick

ISBN: 978-0-578-21154-1 (sc)
ISBN: 978-1-4834-9544-6 (hc)
ISBN: 978-1-4834-9545-3 (e)

Library of Congress Control Number: 2018914817

Lulu Publishing Services rev. date: 01/03/2019

A DEDICATION ...

This work is dedicated to those who have made the biggest positive impact on my journey ...

Rael, my beautiful wife and partner through the better part of my life. She has been one of the most integral parts of my evolution, and she has introduced me to so much wonder in my life ...

Without her, I am nothing ...

Mom, the one who loved me first. The one who gave me breath in my lungs and the wind in my sails. She gave me my life, and showed me how to be.

Eric, my son. My beautiful boy. He taught me how to be a dad and showed me so many different ways to look at absolutely everything. Including how to go on without him ...

Emelie, my daughter. My baby girl. She has helped show me what true strength and courage are. I am honored to be her father.

Without the love and support of them, none of this would even be remotely possible.

There are hundreds of others in my life, human and otherwise, who have given me their time, their energy, and provided me with lessons in this Great Journey. To them, I am grateful for all of the moments shared and blessings given.

An Introduction ...

In each life, there are experiences and moments that can pass unnoticed, and there are ones that make us think, make us act, make us who we are as individuals. The reactions and interactions within these moments, present us with the opportunity to learn and grow ... I have learned to trust the process, no matter the incidence or circumstance. Every moment, every instance, every action, reaction and interaction, defines who we are to ourselves, and to others ...

With this book, I am hoping to be able to share my story and some of the lessons I have learned within the course of 50+ years of life ... The experiences, emotions, thoughts and feelings are all contained within ... Vignettes of the ordinary and the extraordinary, from the perspective of the self ... Some disjointed and scattered, some cerebral and raw ...

All real ...

Everyone has a story to tell ...

My name is Danny, and this is mine ...

ॐ

CHAPTER ONE

Air

9.21.2012 … Friday …

BEH … BEH … BEH … ugh- …

3:15 am – getting up, getting up … coffee first, then feed the cats … good, that's done, now the dogs turn … Brush my teeth, then quietly go in the bedroom to get ready for another day at work … Rael's up … good, I can give her a kiss before I have to go to work. Take my sweatshirt off the hook, start to pull it over my head and … the phone rings.

3:45 am – time stops … it's Bill … He starts by telling me that Mom had a rough night … The nurses and the doctors say they can only make her comfortable at this point. He starts to cry … he knows. I know … We're close … "Bill, it's ok, I am on my way … Love you man. I'm on my way" … click. I set the phone down and tell Rael "I have to go, … I have to go …" Keys, wallet, smokes, lighter – got 'em … "Honey, I love you. Call you soon …" She stops me. "Are you OK..?"

I don't even know at this point …

I have to go do something that I have been preparing two years for …

I am losing my Mom …

I gotta go. Rael hugs me and tells me that it is going to be ok. In the back recesses of my already discombobulated cranial matter, I know that she is right. She lost her Mom, Becky, to cancer..

She knows..

You tell yourself that you are prepared for the eventuality of this; that you are ready.

You Are Not …

I have to go before I fall completely apart … a long drive ahead …

2

The clock says 4:57 …

Driving to Aurora at 5:00 am was never in the plan. I remember watching the dawn break over Aurora, the sky a very deep blue; almost black … I could still see some stars in the pre-dawn sky. I remember thinking: "This isn't real, this CAN'T be real …"

Oh, but it is … it is … Now stop questioning … We have business to attend to …

Right … Gotcha … Admiring the ever brightening colors in the sky.. Dark Purple to Midnight Blue …

Oh, I'm here …

1194 Troy Street.

Where it all began … I grew up here … Thanksgiving, Christmas, Easter, all of them … As I step from my car I pause and gaze at this home, this domain of my childhood. I stood on the front sidewalk for what seemed like an eternity, and smoked the last of my cigarette. In that moment, I was struck by just how quiet it was … Even early in the morning, Aurora, Colorado has a buzz about it … Not this day … I drew the last bit of smoke from my cigarette and flicked it in the street.

Well, this is it …

I walk into the house and stop at the entry. It's quiet … I put my things on the kitchen table, and walk ever so slowly to the back bedroom, where she is … Bill is sitting on the edge of the bed, holding her hand …

She's still breathing, her heart is still beating …

Amazing, considering she survived losing half of a lung a year and a half prior to this moment …

Heart still beating …

3

Bill gets up and motions me to the edge of her bed ... I take her hand in mine, and my entire being, my whole existence is brought in front of me ... She is the one responsible for the man I have become, and creating the foundation for who I am to be ... She ever so slightly squeezes my hand ...

She knows I'm here ...

"Told you we would talk again soon ..."

Still breathing ...

Bill starts to cry and gets up to leave the room. I squeeze her hand and tell her: "I am always going to love you. Forever ..."

Her breaths are starting to get more shallow now ... Bill comes back into the room. I motion for him to sit on the edge of the bed again, and he goes to the head of the bed to hold her other hand ...

Bill – what he has had to endure the last 5 years of his life to this point; basically, taking care of Mom and Dad in that time; the last two years spent taking care of Mom, and helping her through the chemotherapy and, eventually, taking care of her every earthly need as she prepared for her journey home ... He had her help with Dad, two years prior, but now, it fell on him, and, to a lesser extent, me. God Love You, Bill ... He has endured so much ...

It all has come down to this.

I look out her window to see the beautiful colors of the dawn ... We are close now ...

I look upon the face of the of the woman who showed me how to be me, and I glance at the clock in the room ...

6:34 ... So very quiet ...

4

"Thanks for being my Mom … If you need to go, it's alright, we will be alright …" I tell her …

I rise to kiss her forehead … "I love you, Mom.."

As I kiss her on the forehead, a shock goes through me, right through to the floor … and I am filled with light …

6:36 … She has breathed her last.

The most beautiful feeling I have ever experienced has filled me with …"It's going to be OK …"

Margaret Anne Reddick drew her last earthly breath at 6:36 am on September 21st, 2012. No fight, no struggle, just peace, just quiet …

Oh My God … She's gone..!

Bill, silently and stoically, gets up and checks for a pulse and any breath sounds … He turns and starts to cry as he leaves the room. The gentle whirr of the oxygen machine that had become so routine for her, fell silent as the power was turned off. I kissed her head one last time, and rose to leave the room. I glanced back for one final glimpse as I left the room …

Get the List … It's early, but you need to start making calls …

I got the notebook out. In it, is everything that Mom wanted and needed for me to know, specifically for this moment … Bill has all the financial information, for that portion of the program. Mine was how we were going to do the Mass, the music and readings that she wanted, and all of that. I had already called my boss before I ever got to Mom's house, and let him know what was going on. Now the important calls needed to be done. I called Rael first, as she would be the most important call I had to make in this moment. There is something very comforting about calling the one you love, that the one who loved you first, is gone … She asked if I was alright …

It's funny … In that moment, when it's asked, you truly do NOT know if you are OK … When she told me that she loved me, I knew I would be alright …

Just not right now …

Now I had to call "The List", the ones Mom wanted me to call first …

After I spoke to Rael, the first call I made was to Marcus, the youngest sibling … He was well aware of the situation, and was trying to sell his soul to get back to Aurora to be with her, in her final moments … It was my duty, I felt, as the oldest brother, to inform him of Mom's passing …

"Mom drew her last breath about 10 minutes ago …"

The agony on the other end of the line was heart wrenching … "Take care of what you need to take care of," I told him. I always wished that he could have been here for Mom's last moments, and that I could have hugged him in that moment of finality. But, due to his schedule and previous professional commitments, it was not to be. He told me that he would call back later, he needed to book a flight …

The day has dawned …

Rael was the first family to come … She got there right after hospice came to do their final, merciful act for my Mother.

Prepare her for her journey home …

They changed her and made her "presentable", if that's even accurate. We stood in the kitchen: Rael, Bill and I, the only sounds were the ticking of the kitchen clock and a pen scratching on a pad of paper; my Mother's death pronouncement and the inventory of all meds and medical supplies, no longer needed.

"What the fuck am I supposed to do now …??"

I heard it. I said it in my head. All of these emotions, all of these plans: so long in preparation, right down to the music, the church and everything. A plan to be put in motion very shortly, once Marcus comes ... once Marcus comes ...

There's a knock on the front door ...

Two very nicely dressed gentlemen were at the door. Horan McConaty escorts ... I let them in the house. They went over exactly why they were there, and what they needed to do ... They asked permission and my signature to "remove the body" from the premises. I acquiesced and signed the forms. I remember as I was signing this form, that Mom had always said " I will be leaving this house feet first". She was about to get her wish ...

We stood back reverently as they prepared Mom on the gurney, and we watched as they rolled her out, down her hall, past her kitchen, into her front living room; the same living room where Christmases were celebrated; where friends always gathered in happy times and sad, good times and bad ... The two gentlemen told us that they, and the hospice nurses would step outside, to give us all a moment for our final goodbyes ... So surreal, so final, so very REAL. Rael first, then Bill, then me ... I told her that I was gonna love her forever, I kissed her on the forehead one final time and walked out of the room ...

I went into the TV room and stared at the spot that Mom and I used to sit at the picnic table out back, have our cigarettes and talk about nothing ... and everything. I am a coward. I didn't want to watch as my mother was taken out of the house, feet first, for the final time. It was all too much for me to bear. As I looked out at the sun, bathing the backyard on this, the last day of Summer, I heard the wheels on the floor, I heard the front door open and the clack-clack of the gurney wheels going over the threshold of the front door, her final exit from 1194 Troy Street. As soon as I heard the storm door close, I went to the front window to see Bill escorting the gurney to the waiting funereal car; like a centurion, guarding Mom until the very last moment. Fitting really, as Bill had basically become her guardian and caregiver through the final years of her life ... He closed the door to the hearse, put his hand on the back window, and, after a brief moment, they slowly, reverently pulled out of the driveway, and drove down the street … Mom was truly, physically gone … But, oddly, I had an overwhelming sense of peace and tranquility wash over me in those first minutes, standing in the yard, watching the hearse drive away … I never really felt as though she left, spiritually … It was her physical absence that began to get to me. She wasn't gone 5 minutes and I felt like an orphan; a void in my soul, isolated, longing for her presence …

Bill said, "Fuck it … I'm gonna get some beer … I'll be back …" So he did. We sat, we drank, we laughed, we cried, we cried some more … Then Marcus called back.. He found a flight and would be in on Saturday, late afternoon. He wanted to know if he could see her to say his goodbyes …

Now, when the funeral home called earlier in the day, they had asked Bill and I if anyone wanted a viewing, going forward. I told them no, as that was one of Mom's cardinal requests before her passing; NO ONE was to view her after she was gone.

NO ONE … No exceptions …

Sorry Mom … There was no way I could deny Marcus the opportunity to say goodbye to his mother … I can't do that …

The rest of the day is kind of a blur of activity and alcohol. Rael went home to take care of stuff around the farm and meet Emelie when she got home from school. Bill and I sat, drank and basically reminisced about our life. As the afternoon wore on, people started to come by; friends, family, and we all sat outside on this last day of Summer, had some beers, some laughs and some tears. Bill had been up all night with Mom, and had more than a few beers, so I told him to go and get some sleep, or at least some rest. That's when everyone started to show up. And that's why I kept it outside; so he could get some rest. He came outside after a few hours and joined the gathering on the front porch. Talking and remembering, attempting to hold it together …

We have plans to make, gotta include Marcus, but have a lot to do ... The waiting was the worst part of Mom's illness, planning a tribute befitting of this saint of a woman would be the second hardest ... A very close second. We had less than a week to plan, prepare and execute our Mother's Grand Exit, making sure that the ones who mattered, the ones who cared were included and present to say their final goodbyes.

Shit!!! This is gonna be hard ...

How in the world do you put someone's life and what they meant to you, in a service, in a eulogy, in an obituary, giving them a just, fair, and fitting sendoff..? If Bill, Marc and I can just pull this together to do this for her; for us ...

This is gonna be really fucking hard ...

9/22/2012, Saturday

4:30 am, the day after ... Never really got to sleep; still in disbelief and denial. The unbelievable loss and sadness hasn't hit yet ... but its gonna. Well, can't sleep ... might as well get up. Make coffee, feed the cats, the dogs; just like any other work morning, only I don't have to be at work, so ... I keep busy, do chores, clean the kitchen ... Rael's up now ... I get ready to go back to 1194 Troy Street this day, on a mission; putting the pieces together for Mom's funeral. Bill, Marc and I ... Three fuckups ... oh yeah, we can do this ... sure we can ...

I get to the house and Bill is resting, in the TV room. It's quiet ... I open a beer to join him. So starts another blur of a day. Several of Mom's friends stop by to offer condolences. Bill knows every single one. Her friend Mercy, I know, most I do not.. This is all still so unreal to me. We talk, laugh, cry and remember ... Bill doesn't want to be hugged; too hard for him. I get that ... TOTALLY get that ... He doesn't want to be alone. I get that, too.. He is the only family here now, the ONLY one here who understands all the emotions, feelings, and the need to be here more than me. The phone rings several times this day ... Some, Bill answers ... Some, I do ...

Late in the afternoon, the one person I haven't seen in years stops by ... Ivy, my brother Leonard's ex-wife, Ryders mom ... fitting, I think to myself. The one person that all of us hated at one point in our lives. All of us, except for Bill ... and Mom. Mom understood why she left my brother Leonard; understood that she needed to do what she needed to do. For herself, for her son, Ryder. I see that now that I am a dad, a parent ... Clarity comes in this moment. She comes in with food and whiskey ... Good whiskey. Hugs, condolences, and a bite to eat ... She stays briefly while we eat, and drink and reminisce ... The phone rings again; this time it's Marcus ... "Well, it's about fucking time", I think to myself ... It's about time. He tells Bill he will be over "shortly", as he has to get his wife and daughter squared away at his mother-in-law's house, then he'll be over. Ivy stays a little longer and then has to go ... "That was good ..." I think to myself as she pulls out of the driveway.

Two hours pass since Marc has called. Bill and I are sitting at the kitchen table, wondering if he is ok ... He finally decides to show up. No questions if we are ok or not, how we are doing, none of that. He decides to prattle on about how HIS day went, how difficult it was at the airport with the baby, how his daughter was SO difficult to get ready, blah, blah, blah ... "Wow", I think, " Like we really CARE ..." I think it. Bill actually SAYS it. And. Here. We. Go ... Bill, with the help of some really good whiskey, proceeds to tell Marcus all of the things that have been eating at him for the last several years; at HIGH VELOCITY, with MAXIMUM IMPACT ... All I can do is sit there and think, "This is going to get serious real quick.." It's important to note that, when alcohol is introduced into a situation where there is little to no food, even less sleep, and there has been a life and mind altering event, it is simply amazing how much the cranial filters stop working. You start to say things you normally wouldn't say; things that are so vicious and vile, that anyone and everyone within earshot is absolutely stunned ...

"Nobody cares, Marc ... Nobody cares about you or your family or your petty bullshit!!! NOBODY CARES!!!"

Then Marcus does the not-so-bright thing and begins to question Bill, all the while I sit there quiet, and watch all of this unfold before my eyes. And I do nothing. Why..? Because this is them, this has been brewing for quite some time now for reasons that are their own.

Marcus asks Bill, "Why the animosity, Bill..? I was just trying to tell you guys about my day … I thought you would be interested …" I see it before it happens … The redness and anger in Bill's face becomes immediately evident, and somewhere inside my head I hear my Mother: "Let them work it out …" So I sit there.

After some heated back and forth, I explain, somewhat calmly, that right now, we are the only family we have left … We are it. None of any of this has anything to do with what have been asked to do. By our Mother. "If you guys want to kill each other, do it after all of this is over. I don't care. We have to pull it together and do this for Mom." Immediately, calm settles in, and we are again able to concentrate on the task at hand; honoring our Mother.

The rest of the next 4 days was dedicated to this monumental task of making sure absolutely everything was right, and true to everything that our Mother stood for and represented. Her life, her example, her presence was, and still is, so undeniably powerful and magnetic, we wanted to represent her life and her legacy in a manner befitting her. Even though physical death had stilled her voice, I knew that she deserved at least that, and it was up to us to make it beautiful. For Mom.

I took on the honor of writing the eulogy for her, and the text of it is, as follows:

If It's God's Will …

We gather today to celebrate the life and mourn the passing of Margaret A. Reddick. Anne, Mom, Grandma … First, a little obligatory history: Born in Blackstone, Massachusetts on October 3rd, 1933, Anne, born to Fred and Margaret Taylor, spent her formative years in and out of different schools … 13 in 12 years, to be precise, finally settling down with her parents in

Colorado Springs, Colorado. Because of her father's civilian relationship with the military, she met a young Air Force Sergeant, John W. Reddick, with 3 boys of his own. After a brief courtship, she fell in love with "Jack", and they were married in January of 1965. October of '65 saw the birth of their first son together, Danny ... Bill followed in March of 1967, with the baby of the family, Marcus, rounding out the offspring in April of 1970.

Together, we lived at 1194 Troy Street, with summer picnics, street football, huge family Christmases, and living the proverbial "Suburban Dream" ...

When we were coming up, I remember Mom was always keeping busy with her painting and fixing up the yard and the house, as well as working at jobs where she was always helping others, be it handing out meals to the homeless for the holidays, or, in her personal life, talking to innumerable friends and family, offering her advice, counsel and comfort. In every instance and capacity, always considering other feelings and situations before her own. Even in the twilight of her life, as her health was failing, she never stopped asking how everyone else's day was.

The Mother that we knew was fair, but firm; loving, but serious, and she made absolutely sure that we all knew God, and his teachings though the Church, and the Gospels. She exemplified the teachings of Christ in every way giving and caring, loving and sharing, making the absolute best of any given situation ...

Mom's smile could light up an entire country; her laugh, the world ...

Mom and I share a zodiac sign: Libra, and we always balanced each other out. She would tell me if I messed up, as she was always brutally honest that way. That was one of the most wonderful things about who she was as a physical being in this world; her honesty. She helped me learn about our Native American heritage with books and stories passed down to her. You see, she is of Iroquois lineage, out of the Northeastern U.S. and Canada, as are her children. She would show me articles and stories that she had read, and I would reciprocate by having her listen to different types of music that I had "discovered", in an effort to teach, inform, and nurture each others souls ...

"Teach what has been taught", she would tell me. I offer that to you today. Teach what you have been taught and nurture another mind, another soul. We should all try to live by my mothers example, because she loved everyone. No matter societal status, color, race, creed or religion. "If it's God's will", she would say … "Thy Kingdom come, Thy will be done. On Earth as it is in Heaven …"

Even as her illness slowly took away all of the things that she lived to do: gardening, reading, volunteering at St. Andrews, she faced all of it with a strength and grace we should ALL aspire to.

Mom was ready to go home, and early on the morning of September 21st, she took her last earthly breath and was spirited away on the wings of angels, leaving behind, for us, a legacy of love and caring shared by everyone here. THAT is her legacy: a legacy of Love …

I really miss you Mom, but I am supported and strengthened in the knowledge that we will see each other again..

Your Loving Son,
Danny …

CHAPTER TWO

Fire

Personal Evolution: The Journey ...

It is what we make of it. It is what we do with it, and what it does with us. And to us. And around us. The evolution of self is a series of footsteps, a series of events, experiences, days, nights, moments ... Life makes us or breaks us, and it is all part of each of our individual journeys. The physical journey, the mental journey, as well as the spiritual journey each of us is currently on. How we react to each happenstance is a new trail, a new view from the windshield of our eyes. We follow a road map, be it from our hearts, or our minds. This map is comprised of all the different scenarios, or "roads" that this journey leads us to. Every decision, every choice made, every step in any direction leads us on our journey throughout this physical being called life.

Everything within the journey is the catalyst for who we are and who we are to become. From early childhood, taking those first steps into this great big expanse, we are learning. And growing. It is here, as a physical child that we gather the necessary information needed to start the walk of life; words, thoughts, ideas. Simplistic, yes, but they form the start of the pathways that our journey can and will become. This is where the basis for our own Internal/Individual Truth resides. Like any great masterpiece, we start out as a mound of clay; a blank canvas. The pack we carry early on, is light and manageable, as we have only the basics that we need at the beginning of the trek through our lives; simple spiritual nourishment, feelings on a basic level, and the makings of our personality. It is, as we become older and learn more of the life we are leading, as adolescents, that we start to form our own thoughts, our own ideas and concepts about everything we encounter, and start to listen and absorb the thoughts and feelings of those around us. The friends we have, our families, teachers and people in authority, shape and mold our ideas and concepts, directly or indirectly, with their own. In these adolescent years, we are at the whim of the adults in our lives, as they are showing us and telling us about how this journey is supposed to be. From their perspective. Our perspective is a bit more skewed, as we question things, like, why do I have to do that ...? Or why is this the way it should be done ...? We are still in the beginning stages of becoming, so we ask the questions to either: be a smartass, or we genuinely want to know the answer. This is when the purity of simplistic thought starts to get more complicated. We have all of these choices all of a sudden. This, or that, or those … Why do this and not that …? As we start the 'question and answer' period of our youth, we discover harder and more intricate truths. We start to shape our likes and dislikes, good vs bad, and we start to see who, exactly, we can trust. From adolescence through the angst ridden teenage years, and in some cases, early adulthood, our journey and our thought processes are colored and clouded by peer pressure, and doing, saying, liking things because we think it will make us more popular around our friends. Even if some of those things go against our core belief system. It's the friends that matter. It's our individual popularity that matters. Unfortunately, in a lot of cases, the decisions and "truths" that we make in these formidable years, lead to individual confusion, and interior cranial mayhem about what our own, individual internal truth really is.

Do we do things, say things, think things because we want to, or because someone else wants us to ? Do we really believe in our internal truth, with enough conviction to go against the norm and become our genuine true selves?

Are we willing and able to go out on the proverbial limb and think for ourselves, and "damn the torpedoes", not giving a second thought to what others may say?

The search for our own individuality continues, I believe, throughout our entire lives, but who we are, at least essentially, doesn't really become part of our soul, until we reach 'full on' adulthood. When we determine, finally determine, what our life path is to start to become, then, and only then can we examine who we are by all of our past experiences. For some, this happens when they get married, others when there are children entered into the mix, still others when they lose someone close, either when they move away, or when their life ends, or the end is near. Each of the above has helped me in the realization of who I am, and who I am to be. When I asked my wife to marry me, I had to wrap my entire existence around the fact that I had to think for others outside myself now. My own interests now, had to become secondary in that, I now had to think on much less of a "me" level, and more on an "us" level. Compromise, consideration, and carefully weighing all options in every aspect of my life, had to become the primary goal and focus. When my daughter was born, that solidified all of the thinking behind doing for others first. Protect and defend the others, at all cost. There were now others who depend on me, and I was no longer the "be all, end all" ... I looked to my mother for some of the answers, and deeper within for others. This is when the need to look back on my life first took hold. The actions of myself, and the reactions of my parents, didn't seem so crazy now ... And as my son, who was 5 at the time, started to do things that 5 year old's do, I was brought back to my youth, and looked at both sides of the parental equation; Mom's and mine. And, because I was raised the way I was, the only male fatherly influence I really had was my dad's example: The Fear of God technique. Instill the fear of God into the children, and MAKE them respect you. Needless to say, that did not work very well with Eric. It worked well with me, because I was, more or less, afraid of the old man. Eric, even at an early age, had ideas about where he wanted to be in life, and was very self-assured, so he wasn't intimidated by anyone. So I had to understand and comprehend that, for starters. And it was inherent upon me, to take a different direction with my son, in his upbringing and trying to instill trust with him. I had to learn a different way to parent, from the way I was "parented" by my dad. I decided to take the direction of my Mother's parenting example. Listen, be fair, DO NOT JUDGE, and above all else, show them that their interests MATTER. I don't have to like what my kids like, but I will show an interest in what they are interested in. That, I found out, is a great way to open up the lines of communication between generations. It also helped me open my mind to the wonderfulness of new things for me. Music, art, ideas that would never have occurred to me before ... New roads, new thought patterns, different colors on the journey. I am eternally grateful for my son, because his individuality showed me a different course, a different road to take as a father. And him and I became a lot closer because of it. He showed me new, unexpected roads to take; detours from the normal path. Detours that, in the moment, were scary, but oh so beautiful and fulfilling.

In losing someone close, we are able to look at our lives, our journey up to this point, from a more raw and primal perspective. When they move away, we look at our road travelled with them with fondness and wish them well in their journey going forward, hoping at some point in this physical existence, that our paths will cross again. We hear from them from time to time, checkpoints in the dual journeys, to catch up and reminisce about times gone by. In this part of the journey, there is always a hope that our physical paths will meet again. When someone in our journey dies, especially if that "someone" is a close friend or relative, the journey comes to a temporary halt. Even, in some cases, if that someone is a four-legged family member. Everything comes to a stop.

When my father died, because he was the way he was, I only reflected briefly, with little to no grief in the loss. Selfishly, I was angry, because I never got to verbalize to him, just what I was feeling all through my youth, and that anger festered inside for quite a long time. Then, Mom died, and the one who loved me first, was gone from this physical plane. Dad died rather suddenly, and it was a relief, more than a loss. Mom was different, as we had time to talk about absolutely everything, and, while we didn't have a concrete date, we knew that our time together was limited. So we talked. And talked. We had heart to heart discussions about absolutely everything under the sun, and in that time, I got to know my mother on the most sacred and spiritual level; finding out things I never even knew about the woman who raised me. It was also in this time, that her final wishes were discussed, ad infinitum. How she was to be taken care of after she passed, the celebration, and who to notify on the day of her death. All of it. And when she passed, I felt that spiritual side of her flow into me. I missed her physical presence, and still do, but there is a calm in my soul. The day she died, my life, my consciousness, my journey was altered forever, as I now felt orphaned. In the physical sense. In the spiritual realm, I have felt more focused, more in tune, if you will, because I know she is right here with me. Since the day I was born, she has been right here, with me. Little did I know at that time, that my journey would take another incredible turn, into a place that I had never been before. This part of the journey has had the largest and most difficult and direct impact on every aspect of my entire existence. Everything I thought I believed in, was shattered to the core.

December 28, 2015.

The darkest day of my entire life, and the day the journey stopped, in it's tracks. The day my son died. Rael and I found him. I remember looking at his face and I remember not being able to breathe, to think, to do anything in that instant. I remember his mother's horrifying scream, thinking in that instant, that, this was a complete and utter disaster, of biblical proportions. And, regrettably, I was right. In that moment, 50 years of the journey, everything I thought I believed, everything I stood for, everything I felt and knew, was reduced to a smoldering pile of rubble. Dazed, I looked around *inside my head*, and saw nothing but black smoke and the charred remains of everywhere I had been in my life up to that moment. In that moment everything was burning to the ground. Everywhere I looked, devastation. Stripped to the bare bones of my existence, this was a true and complete Ground Zero. I don't remember who called 911, as there are parts of that moment that are foggy. Trying to absorb all of this, I do remember seeing Rael holding him, weeping so deeply that I thought I was going to lose her in that moment as well. Mind racing, not even beginning to know what to do, where to go, how to breathe, nothing ... In the next few hours, all I remember is concentrating on Rael; making sure that she was going to remain upright, and trying, miserably, to keep her calm through what had just transpired. I also needed to make sure that I remembered absolutely everything from this terrible day, for reference. As the Peru trip took me on such an absolutely beautiful soul journey, this one was exactly the opposite. From when we found him, to the people coming by to offer condolences, to his memorial service, it was like my entire being was stuck and sinking in quicksand. The blessings throughout this time, were the people who came and listened, who came and stayed here, making sure we were never alone. So much to absorb in that short time, the initial shock wore off after a while, and we were left with the pain; the anguish of trying to be able to function now as a family of 3, where there used to be 4 ... His feline children, who were with him in his last moments, came to live here. They were every bit as terrified, if not more, about the prospect of not having their dad physically around anymore. In these difficult moments, we knew that we had to be there for them, more, I think, than for ourselves. They were ripped from what they knew and loved, into a world of dogs, of noises they weren't used to, people they didn't know; a world of extreme uncertainty for them. We showed them that they were going to be accepted here, as part of the family, as all animals in our realm are. We had them live in Emelie's room for the first couple of weeks after they came here, if only for a chance to feel secure and safe within this strange new existence. Slowly, almost methodically, they began to venture out of her room, into this new, strange expanse, getting to acclimate themselves to the new beings around them. And as we slowly, almost methodically began to come out of our extreme darkness, their light helped to show us light in our lives as well. As the fog started to lift and people went back to their lives and existences, we were left to attempt to do the same. In each moment, the realization sank in deeper, the emotions started to wane, and, in these moments, I started to look back on my life. I started the retrospective of who, what, where, and why I have been the way I have been. In looking back, I could at least start, to look forward. To heal. To try and live again. The rubble was still all there, but I could see growth, and I was able to start on the journey again. The myriad of lessons and teaching points in that time, were endless and boundless. I started to look at the people I had in my life in that time, and see if they were conducive to my personal growth. I soon came to realize that a lot of the friends I had for the better part of my life, were nowhere to be found in our time of greatest need. I also discovered another harsh truth; the family that was there through all the good and happy times, also felt the need to disappear in this time as well. It hurt, but only for a moment. The realization that the family I needed by my side was already here, made all of it seem ok. And it is ok. Why..? Because my wife and my daughter are the only ones who have any inkling of what I have gone through, and I, them. They are the only ones who have helped me the most on this part of the journey, holding me up and keeping me moving forward, even when I didn't feel like moving forward. Sure, I have friends that help me through sometimes, when the going gets a little rough, but for the most part, they are at a distance, either in a different state, or ones that don't communicate as often. That is also ok, because they are the friends that understand. They get it, and in some cases, they are travelling the same road that we are. And in the journey we are all on, that is enough ... We will keep going ...

Wish you were here..

Dearest Eric,

In the weeks and months since you departed, we have been a part of something that has altered our very existence forever ... The sheer pain of losing you, individually and collectively as a family, has left us with a void that would be impossible to fill ... on ANY level ... You were, and will remain, a better man than I could ever hope to be ... The compassion and genuine interest that you showed with absolutely everyone, is a trait that is lacking infinitely in our society ... You took the time to educate, you took the time to listen, you took the time to give a shit ...

And everyone that we have talked to in this time, has affirmed for us what we already knew: that our son was special ... These people, from absolutely everywhere, joined us for your Celebration, to help the family, the community start to heal ... These people; your friends from school, your boys, their parents, people you worked with, so many people who took time out of their day to offer us, US, condolences on our loss ... Visits, phone calls, emails.. ... from everywhere ... You touched so many lives by just being there and caring, and sharing a part of yourself with each and every one ...

We have known for many years that you were, and still are, very special to us ... Attitudes and lessons that you imparted to us in your ever too brief stay here, will continue to permeate the very fiber of our home, our life, our existence ...

I am proud to be your dad, Eric ... My admiration for all you achieved while you were here, knows no bounds ... You stuck to your principles, and stayed true to yourself, doing so with dignity and honor to your name ... and our family ...

We miss you, son, and we will love you until the end of time ...

Your loving dad ...

P.S.

Call your mother …

December 28, 2015 … One Year Ago …

On this day our entire lives were altered in a way that nothing has before. At the age of 27 earthly years, he was called to a different plane; another existence, away from the trials and tribulations that this physical existence held for him …

In this time, we have had to learn to live without our beautiful boy; our loving, caring, ever evolving human son … In this time, we have had to deal with all of the emotions, memories and lessons that such a personal and profound tragedy entail for those of us left behind … I cannot, and will not speak for his sister or his mother, as that is, and will not be my place. The only place that I can speak from is my own heart; my own place …

Dearest Eric,

The past year has been a journey of monumental proportions from every side of absolutely every spectrum within this life without your life. I am eternally grateful for your presence and absolutely devastated by your absence. I have tried, as your father, to impart wisdom and knowledge to you, as you were growing up, in becoming a man. In that, I have learned far more from you than I could ever attempt to teach you. You have opened my eyes to the many wonders of the natural world outside of this place we call home … I have learned how to be a better human being; a being with consciousness, a being of energy and of light. You introduced me to new ways of thinking, new ways of doing, and new ways of listening and seeing. You have had and will continue to have vision and wisdom far older than the 27 years you blessed us with while you were here on this big blue marble … I am trying to become a better man, a better being through all of the lessons that you imparted to me while you were here, and the lessons that I continue to learn in your physical absence.

In life, you became, not only my son, but also my best friend, a very trusted advisor in all things physical, musical, and ethereal.

In your departure I have learned so much more about who "Eric" was, and continues to be.. I will continue to live my life in the same pursuit of excellence, pride in others, and genuine honesty and dignity, that seemed so effortless to you … I will attempt to continue your legacy of teaching and showing, with the utmost respect and compassion that you carried in this, the physical realm. I miss you in every moment of every hour of every day, and will continue to do so, until we meet again, on the other side. I will continue to wear the color blue in your honor, with honor and respect for everything you have done, continue to do, and everything that you mean to me.

I am proud of the man that you became, and the spirit that you continue to be, and I will always, ALWAYS be proud that you are my son.

My son.

You have made me a better human being, and I am honored to be your dad.

I love you Eric …

Every minute,

Every hour,

Every single day.

#blue4eric

#celebrateeric

#alwaysremembereric

This time ...

As the world prepares for the holiday season, no matter what you celebrate, stores, malls, restaurants, highways and byways are filled with people, rushing to buy that perfect gift for all of those special someones in their lives ... The preparation for a house filled with those who mean the most; the day when love, laughter and stories of holidays past permeate the air ... Usually in this time, thoughts drift back to when I was a child/young adult and the time spent with my parents, grandparents and the extended family; kids outside playing street football, adults in the house either watching whatever football game happened to be on, or sitting in the kitchen with wine and conversations far too boring for the kids to handle ... Even as I got older, the football games in the street were shared with the conversation around the kitchen table; remembrances of Christmas past, learning at least a little bit about the past and the traditions and values of a society before I came to be ...

When I had my own family, some of the traditions from our combined families melded together to form new ones ... Some of the old ways for the parents managed to survive; staying up until after midnight, making sure the kids were asleep before we could break out the gifts from Santa, with handwritten notes to them. Getting up at 4:00 Christmas morning to the excitement and sheer joy that only the expectation of "what Santa brought me" can bring.. Exhausted, we would sit on the couch with coffee, and revel in their excitement, watching as those little faces would light up with each new discovery, each new addition to their stash ...

These are memories that bring a small sense of warmth, peace and serenity to us this Christmas.. This year, we will spend the holidays just us.. together in a quiet space, a serene place, unencumbered by gifts and expectations. ... It will be far less than a celebration, but more a reflection and meditation on everything we have experienced in the last year.

It will be our first Christmas without decoration, without expectation, and most importantly, without our Eric ... December 25th will be, going forward, a time for reflection; a time to spend together, as a family, and just be … In this time, we are the gift to each other, in this time, we will hold each other up, ever moving forward, ever growing …

In this time …

Blue4Eric …

We chose this as our rally cry for the memory of, and legacy left, by our son, Eric. So, two days a year we will celebrate his life, his legacy, his mark on our lives as his family. May 24th, the day we were graced with his physical presence, and December 28th, the day we embraced his spiritual essence. I wear blue every single day, as a beacon of hope to my soul. I have found that the mere act of wearing blue has helped to calm my spirit and focus myself in this maddening world we live in. It has helped me calm myself in times of struggle, frustration and consternation. Blue was his favorite color, and it is a representation of calmness, tranquility and spirituality, at least for me. I will wear blue for the rest of my days on this earth, because I don't want anyone to forget the power of remembrance of someone you love.

Blue has that power.

As his father, it was my duty, my obligation, my PRIVELEDGE to impart wisdom upon this young man, so that when he became a young adult man, he would have, at least in part, a pathway into adulthood. Not surprisingly, he became his own man, his own individual self, with his own identity, and sense of self-worth. As much as I had imparted upon him, he reciprocated the knowledge a million times over. He challenged my way of thinking, and presented different ideas, a different structure to the knowledge presented to me as I grew up. The ideas and structures we discussed, at great length, have become a part of who I have become as an individual, and have helped me realize the absolute vastness and beauty of everything, not just in my little corner of this planetary plot of land.

Dearest Eric,

On this, the anniversary of your birth, I wanted to let you know how proud I am to be your dad. Through all of the good times and bad, you never, ever lost faith in me, and were, and continue to be, instrumental in keeping me upright. I only wish that you would have had more time in this physical realm, as there are so many things that I wanted to do with you and say to you, and I just miss having you around. In the time since you have been gone, life has gotten hard at times, but your Mother, sister and I have pushed onward. Ever onward, safe in the knowledge that we will all see you again.

May 24th may not have been such a huge deal to you as an adult, but to us, it was the day that an unequaled gift was bestowed upon us. We will continue to honor your memory, your life and your legacy as a gift to the world. You have made an impact on everyone who came in contact with your physical being, and you continue to impact us immeasurably, as we go forth in our lives. I will continue to tell people of what we have talked about, and attempt to touch as many lives as you did, in your brief time here. You have always mattered to me, and I will forever be grateful for everything that you have showed me, taught me, and shared with me.

Happy Birthday, Son.

I miss you every single day, and I will always love you.

Dad ...

The Girls ... His Girls ...

For as far back as I can remember, there have always been "house pets" in my life ... Be it a dog, or a cat or even a goldfish, this is how I was taught responsibility ... As I have gotten older, I have realized that the animals that cohabitate with us here, are not "house pets" ... They are so much more, in every sense ... They are members of the family and, in my estimation, very vital to the health and welfare of the human members of this household ... On this little patch we call home, it is almost a given that any and all animals that happen to stop by, will always, ALWAYS be safe within the confines of these 4 fences ... I believe in the power of not only the human soul, but of the animal spirits as well, and, in my experience, the animal spirits hold a somewhat greater power than their human counterparts ...

When Eric's spirit was freed into the vast, he left a legacy that, in my opinion, will only continue to grow and bloom ... As part of the living legacy that he left in this physical world, we have been honored and blessed with the inclusion of Thea and Isis to our family ... And, as that living legacy, they are not merely cats; they are, for all intents and purposes, our grandbabies. ... Think what you will, but because our son raised, cared for, and worshiped these girls, and because they were with him as he drew his last earthly breath, they will always, ALWAYS be an extension of Eric ... Thea and Isis have seen and been through so much in the last year, with all of the changes and the uprooting their entire existence, into an entirely new and different place, people, other animals, and wide open spaces ... As the days and weeks passed since they arrived, slowly, cautiously, methodically, they began to explore this new set of surroundings, careful not to let any of us see, or come anywhere near them ... and we let them be ...

As the weather started to get warmer, and the days started to get longer, they explored farther within the house, occasionally making eye contact, but staying just out of arms reach ... I took a leap of faith on a warm March day, and opened the front door to see how they would react ... I thought for sure that would be the last time that I would see them, but they needed to get outside and breathe again ... Feel the sun on their faces and the breeze in their fur again ... Eric took them outside all the time, for walks and hikes behind his apartment complex ... Not completely unexpectedly, they spent the majority of that Saturday outside, but, never ventured out any further the front yard ... As the sun started to set, as we were on the front porch, both girls came up and went to the front door and sat ... I slowly walked to the front door, hoping against hope that they wouldn't turn and bolt ... They didn't ... I opened the front door and, meowing softly, they went in the house, and back to "their" room, where they summarily passed out from the days activities ... Since that day we have been able to get close to them; to bond with them, a mutual trust and love evolving ... We love and have always loved all of the animals that have shared our spaces with us, but these two ... These two have captured us in a way that I would have never thought possible ... I hope and pray Eric approves of how we are raising his kids ...

Our grandchildren ...

His Jeep ...

After he passed, it was decided that, because this Jeep was one of Eric's cherished earthly possessions, we would keep it in our stead ... He took this everywhere, and I mean EVERYWHERE ... He beat the shit out of it, going camping, fishing, hiking, everywhere in the Colorado High Country ...

His students gave him a hard time about the color, calling it his Barbie Jeep ...

After more lengthy discussions, it was also decided that we would do all of the work and modifications to it that Eric wanted ... The entire suspension was the most expensive on the list so it was the first thing ... That piece is now complete as we got it back from the shop today, and I will be driving it as my primary driver now ...

We wanted to have it painted Candy Apple Blue, like Eric and I discussed in his last Summer, but due to an accident, we had it painted the original Teal ...

It may not be much, but it was his, and we want this to be what he wanted ... I am humbled and honored to drive it ...

It still smells like him ...

The best father's days gifts I have EVER received were the sacred gift of my children ...

Eric and Emelie ...

Thank you both for teaching me and letting me help guide you in our time together ...

Thank you for sharing at least a small part of all of this craziness with me ...

I am extraordinarily proud to be your Dad ...

I will love you both until the end of forever ...

Primal ... Redux ...

Pain ... Searing, white hot, burning to the primal core.. This, too, has become an abject, very real lesson in survival ...

Emotional, spiritual, psychological, and physical survival. ... Of the self, and of the family ...

I have become a little more keenly aware of my surroundings when I am away from here ... more so with Rael and Emelie ...

When I am out with the animals, or when we went on our nature walk, listening to what the wind, or the rustle of the grass has to say ... Now that it's getting warmer, more outside treks within the larger journey, will be planned ... To listen, to be, to decompress, to see and envelope the soul in all that is outside ...

The everyday can be so overwhelming sometimes ...

Something as simple as the sun on your face in the morning, can change an entire headspace ...

Thoughts, prayers and remembrances of Eric, are the sun on the face of my soul ...

Go outside when it's quiet, and listen ... just listen ... and reconnect ...

May 24th, 1988 ...

And on this day, a son is born ...

A birth that would change more than a few paths on this trek ...

A birth and a life that inspired so many different levels of feeling and different levels and ways of thinking about absolutely everything..

A life, that, like a gentle spring rain, touches and nourishes everything ...

An individual that has given me the education that I needed to become a good father, a good man and a good human being ...

Eric helped me when he was younger, by testing my patience; attempting in some way to teach me tolerance ... It worked ...

I think back to birthday parties past; Discovery Zone, the lizard guy, camping and sunburns with a side of downpours on the Arkansas River, fishing last year. ... There were some rough times, as there sometimes is, but we always got through ... as a family. Many more, were the good times, and they were great ...

Eric,

We love you Son ... Although you were taken from us entirely too soon, your presence is still felt within the confines of our home, and within our hearts ... We always tried, as parents, to give you the absolute best of everything that we could, and the way that you turned out as a young man is validation that "you are a good boy" ... Your mother and I are so very proud of everything you have done, and everything that you have brought to this family and our existence ...

On a personal note, I would like to thank you helping me when I needed it, for showing me different ways of thinking; of being, of believing ... I miss you every moment of every day, but your presence helps keep me going ... Thank you for everything you were and everything you are; a very intense transfer of energy and light ...

Happy Birthday Eric ... We will love you until the end of forever ...

... an admiration ...

As a father, I cannot even imagine what it is like to be a mother. Let's start with childbirth. As males we flit around and do our own thing, while the mother-to-be feels all of the things an expectant mother feels psychologically, physically, spiritually, all the while nurturing this child inside. As the father-to-be, all we can do is attempt to make our significant other more comfortable, not really understanding at ALL the dynamic of child birth. When that momentous day arrives and it's time for the baby to come, we, as males, puff out our chest and proclaim to the world that we are going to be a father ... Real big talk from someone who is NOT going through the obvious pain and discomfort that is childbirth. Males of ANY species cannot truly appreciate the entirety of motherhood, even a little. After watching what my mother went through raising us, I gained a little bit of an appreciation for what mom's go through. It wasn't until Rael and I were blessed to have children, that I TRULY got an understanding of what motherhood entails. I have seen the good, the bad, the happy, and the sad. And I have seen a pride in her children that is unmatched by any father.

ANY father ...

And while I KNOW that I have not always been the most considerate, most attentive, or most understanding individual on the planet, I have a tremendous amount of love, respect, and admiration for everything that she, as our children's mother has gone through, and continues to go through every minute, of every hour, of every day …

The sacrifices she has had to make, on every level, at every turn; the strength that she has had, and continues to have, and the absolute love that she has for her children is something that I can only hope to attain …

When you are a mother, dedication and protection of your children is absolutely first on the list. I can't even begin to express my gratitude for the way she has raised the kids. She has given them their sense of self, of being an individual, and how to be strong in the face of adversity.

Rael,

You have faced many adversities in our time together, a great deal of them caused by me, but I want you to know that I am grateful for all you have done and continue to do for Emelie, and everything, EVERYTHING that you have done and continue to do for Eric and the preservation of his memory and legacy … I am sorry I haven't been "here" as much as I absolutely should have been, but please know that you will always have my undying respect and gratitude for everything you have done, and all you continue to for our children …

Happy Mothers Day.

I will love you until my last breath.

That day in December and the aftermath …

Our son died on Monday …

I won't say how, or why, or offer any kind of explanation or conjecture …

All I know right at this very moment is this world lost a shining light, and the most honest example of a good man … Eric was a good man, a kind man, a wonderful example of a human being, and quite simply the best son a man like me could ever want, need, or have … Words cannot begin to express our family's profound sorrow and grief at this time, and we respectfully request our privacy in helping us to grieve as a family …

I love you, son. … I always will …

A life, a family can go from the absolute peak of joy and harmony at Thanksgiving and Christmas, and have every last little bit of everything of and for this life, ripped away in a moment … A moment … Everything has changed …

I have learned that this life affected more than just the ones related to him … This life affected others who, in turn, affected us by the love and caring shown to him in so many wonderful, truly touching ways … I am humbled by your compassion and generosity, and genuine caring as we attempt to move in a forward direction..

We have talked and decided that as far as alpaca shows go, we will more than likely be sending a few of our animals to a couple of shows, but we will not be attending any shows this year as exhibitors … That being said, we may come as spectators, depending on ten million different variables …

I have learned that the pile of bullshit and the portfolio of what is truly important to me, is now more proportionally accurate. … The circle has gotten smaller and somewhat easier to carry in case of emergency, if you will … Same goes with the people … If you are reading this, there's a good chance you are part of the portfolio and not the pile.. The ones who give a shit and care … Grazie …

I have learned, for now at least, that I communicate better when I write … I simply cannot go to a crowded area and attempt to have small talk … I do at work, because Rael is there, and, as a consultant for her company, it would be in our best interest to at least attempt to play nice … So I do … Small, work related talk … That's it … I am comfortable here, with the herd, the family, the peace and quiet at 0300 … I have texted people and asked them not to call me, because I can't.. I just can't …

I have learned that when this life, this force of nature in so many ways, was stilled [at least here in the physical sense], a large part of ourselves was quieted as well ...

And I am really not quite sure how to fucking handle that. ...

There is a place here on the farm where I go ... Its dark there and quiet, no distraction ... Three o'clock in the morning, and I listen ... hoping for a whisper in the wind ... I will take the solace ...

I have learned that the animals understand the emotion, and the consequence, and they act and react accordingly ... I have learned that they can express compassion and care to those of us human beasts in our time of emotional, psychological, and spiritual distress ... They are there watching over us, and keeping us in sight-lines at all times ... Dogs, Llamas, all of them ... Homeland security ...

I have learned, that the more I learn about my son, the more I want the entire world to know about him ... I want the world to see that true success and notoriety can be achieved, not by the size of your ego or your bank account, rather by the size of your heart, the amount of honor and sincerity you have towards another being, human or otherwise, the commitment to THEIR success and not his own. ... I want the world to know how he taught so many young minds, not just the intricacies of gymnastics, but some of the intricacies of life, of living, of being; imparting a part of himself on them, to them ... Eric is always one to look out and not look in ... Their successes are theirs and he reveled in them ... His success came in their learning and growing and getting more confident in who they are and where they're going ... There were no problems, only opportunities to do better ... That's what I want the world to know ... That my son was, and is, a good man ... He was, and is, a man of great honor, who carried himself with grace and dignity no matter who was in the room ... That's what I want the world to know ...

Peace ...

On behalf of my wife and daughter, I would like to thank all of the wonderful people who have sent words of condolence, and words of inspiration … As parents we always hope that we can make a positive impact in our children's lives, and they, in turn, can make a positive difference in the life of someone else … We have been shown over the last 2 days, through responses on Facebook and externally, that our son, our beautiful boy, helped make a difference in the lives of so many … We are tremendously grateful to all who have reached out with words, and deeds, to help us navigate through this very dark, very saddened time for all of us … It shows me, as a father, that my son was well thought of, loved, and was able to impact others in the most positive way … Thank you all so much … You are a blessing to us …

28 days …

Not a whole lot of time in the grand scheme of things … In that space of time though, fates can change, an entire course derailed …

The last 28 days have brought me realizations about everything I ever thought I believed in, everything I thought I would experience in MY lifetime, and it has brought something else …

Pain …

A pain I could never imagine in my worst nightmare. … I always thought that after Mom died in 2012, that THAT would be the worst feeling I would ever have to experience …

I was wrong …

Mom's was expected and followed the natural order of things in the universe …

This, though … This is some omnipotent beings version of a really fucked up joke …

Every single fiber of my being has been on heightened alert since, ever protective of my wife and child ... Grown women to be sure, but I am who I am ...

Trying to keep my tenuous hold on the sanity I have left ... Keeping it together, for the good of the many, in the name of the one ...

I never, ever want to feel this pain ever again ... Ever ...

This is 10,000 lifetimes of pain seared into 28 days ...

In 28 days I have met people and connected and reconnected with souls that joined with Rael, Emelie and I in our time of sorrow ... These people, these angels of mercy, were, and continue to be there, to help us try and navigate this part of the journey ... And for them, we are ever grateful ...

The journey continues, ever onward, one day, one moment at a time ...

Keep Moving ...

This past weekend we took on the task of getting all of our son's physical property together and boxing it up, for storage ... It's amazing the entire gamut of emotions that run through every cell of your being, as you go through 27 years of a life and put it, quite unnaturally, away ... Sifting through and finding memories and moments, accomplishments and awards, drawings and sketches, grocery lists and cd liner notes ... Work shirts and play shirts, t-shirts from vacations long ago ...

They still smelled like him ...

It was sacred, going through this virtual museum of our son's existence, from birth to rebirth ...

As we sorted and boxed and stacked all of the boxes and took apart the bedroom, we noticed that this place of his, this domain and sanctuary for him and his cat's, his "girls" as he called them, was now nothing more than a collection of walls and a roof ... His earthly possessions stacked and arranged neatly in the middle of the living room.. We left this place with a sense of accomplishment, but also an enormous sense of sorrow for the needful that we had to do ...

We have rented a box truck, and have procured a storage space here in Elizabeth to store his things until we can be able to go through them properly ...

We are planning to move all of his possessions this Saturday at 10:00 am ... I implore any and all of my friends, Facebook and otherwise, to please help us load and move all of the furniture and boxes from his place in Castle Rock to the storage unit in Elizabeth ... If you can spare a half day on Saturday to help us with this final step, the temporary resting place for his things ...

All we need is some able bodied individuals to assist us with moving and cleaning ...

The response to our call for help was absolutely amazing ... We had so many people from so many places and spaces come and help us with the needful ...

Today we moved all of our sons things into a concrete storage unit here, close to us ...

Something we never thought, in a million years, that we would ever have to do ...

But we did it ... With the help, compassion and genuine kinship of souls; a group dedicated to a single purpose and a single goal ...

At 10 am sharp, people came and asked where they were needed ... No task too great or menial ... Rael and I were a wreck ... going through making sure we remembered everything, and people filing in and out, quietly, reverently grabbing things and loading them into the truck ... All I was able to do was straighten some things out in trailer ... Everyone else grabbed and started loading ... Others who came at 1015 or so, asked

to help Rael with the cleaning and final once over of Eric's apartment. …
The truck was loaded and we went to the storage unit, and the most eerily
reverential thing I have ever witnessed occurred …

We got to the storage unit here in town and there were 5 cars behind me in
line … I didn't realize until we drove in that they followed me for the un-
load … We got to the unit and I pulled the truck up to the door and pulled
the ramp out … As I opened the door to the storage unit, a quiet procession
started, and my sons earthly belongings were being brought into this place
to reside, at least temporarily … One by one we grabbed boxes and tables
and furniture and brought them inside … without a word … Marty got a
lock for the back door, thank you Marty. … My gratitude. … We closed
the door, had a group smoke, and went on about our Saturday …

Saying thank you to all of you would have proved impossible for me today,
but now, on reflection on all of it, I can say that we are blessed … Blessed
in that we have people in our lives, who, like Eric, actually give a shit. …
We collectively, and I personally, am grateful and extremely humbled by
this entire experience, as the caring and compassion of certain humans on
this planet, has given me hope. … Our son did good in his life, and it is
and was beautiful to see the same attitude within the group who had never
met before today..

The ones who knew Eric out there in the big wide world, in HIS personal
life, we have become acquainted with, and all of them, and all of you who
knew him, have given his Mother and I a look into the man he became …
In his own right. … On his own terms …

I thought I was proud of him before … man. … To know him is to love
him, and to love him is beautiful … .

Through the silence comes clarity … Clarity of remembrance, of purpose,
of tradition … Our family will carry the legacy forward … Of kindness,
of learning and growing and teaching and showing … To teach, educate,
grab that brass ring, and move ahead,,, Forward is going to take some time
yet … Still very raw, not quite real …

Standing on the porch, having a smoke, its dark ... .and still. ... no wind, or traffic, or dogs barking ... nothing. ... and through the quiet, clarity ...

Peace ...

On behalf of the Reddick family, we would like to thank the hundreds of people who joined us yesterday for Eric's Celebration of Life. We are humbled and blessed to have had all of the wonderful friends, family, and Eric's gymnastics team join us for an afternoon of love, of unity, of stories, of life ... You are all a blessing to us in this time of tremendous sorrow ... Several people shared their memories with all of us during the Celebration, including myself. Below are the words I read for our son, in tribute to the man, the coach the brother, the son ...

For the last 12 days, we have received messages on Facebook, email as well as letters and cards, and people have gone out of their way to come and see us, and we are humbled to the core by the absolute outpouring of compassion and shared communal grief over the loss of our son. Words cannot begin to express our deep appreciation and gratitude for all of you and many more who have been here, either at the house, on the phone, or otherwise ... We love you guys..

....

There are people in our lives who just get by, lurking underneath the radar, keeping their head down, trying to not get noticed ... There are others who are all about the "look-at-me" factor, where everything they do, absolutely MUST get noticed and praised, glorifying themselves and their accomplishments to anyone who will listen ... Then there are those extremely rare individuals, who exhibit the best of both worlds, doing the best that they can, not for the personal accolades, but for the betterment of the other individuals, within the team, and within the community ...

My Son, Eric, was just such a man ...

From a young age, we knew our son was going to do what he was passionate about ... As it turns out, he had several pursuits that he excelled at tremendously: fishing, guitar, gymnastics … His true passion lay beneath the surface of all of these things: Eric, to the core, was an educator; a mentor, a shaman, if you will … His thirst for knowledge was insatiable, and his knack and need for imparting that knowledge was just as insatiable. He made himself smarter by teaching others, showing others, being with others and becoming genuinely interested in their BEING, not just their day … He and I could sit around and discuss consciousness versus social consciousness, or the last episode of Family Guy, it didn't matter. He had the ability to be able to talk to anyone, and have a genuine interest in what they had to say …

It wasn't always that way …

Mostly a loner when he was young, he thrived in the great big outdoors at Nana's farm in Sedalia. Doing what boys want to do; catch frogs, find arrowheads, go on a long explore … He learned about nature and the harmony within, from being on her farm … 80 acres of complete heaven for an active little man, this is where he was the most comfortable. As evidenced, in his later explorations, by his love of fishing and hiking and just listening to the conversations among the Aspens in Como on a warm autumn day … All the synapses firing, the colors, the smells, the textures of life, all right there in front of him …

Eric never really conformed to the idea of strict, in your face, book learning. Don't get me wrong, he was a voracious reader as he got older, but he was learning things he WANTED to learn, not what he was being TOLD to learn. Prone to listening to podcasts on world history and the ramifications of World War One on today's society … This was something that he wanted to know about, so he found it, and he learned about it … All of it … How do I know this..? He told me about it.. At Thanksgiving dinner … But this is how he was; always thinking, always making others think … Continuous learning experiences, in every situation. He would always say " … but, you know, … if you THINK about it …".. Constantly challenging himself and the others around him, to make himself better, and, maybe, just maybe, the others around him would become better as well.

I know I am …

He was not only my son, but he also imparted a lot of wisdom to me as well … Eric is and was an old soul, with conventional wisdom of people twice his age … This is what I will miss … The discussions, the talks, the rare fishing trip that took us to the remotest places in Colorado when it was just him and I and the glory of all creation around us …

We may not have caught anything, but I always told him that the time we spent together meant more to me than any fish … No matter how big …

Eric,

I miss you, son … I miss your smiling face coming in the front door, guitar case in hand on a random Sunday … I will miss the podcasts on everything to religious traditions of ancient Croatia, to the Russian involvement in World War I, and the discussions that ensued … I miss your laugh, both when you were little and as a grown man … I miss the glow on your face when you show us the progress of the boys team, every step of the way, in preparation for the next meet … on your phone … I miss wrestling with you in the kitchen while your mother was cooking dinner … I miss watching you snowboard, gliding so effortlessly across the snow, navigating everything so precise, so perfectly … I miss kissing you on the head and telling you that I love you … because I do, you know … I am tremendously honored and humbled to be your father, as you are, by FAR, the best ex-ample of a man that I have EVER known … The way you carried yourself and your complete investment in absolutely everything you hold dear is where I aspire to be within my existence … Your loyalty and dedication to our family and to the people you hold dear, is an ideal that is true to your heart … I am very proud of the man that you have become, and I am proud to be your Dad …

We love you so very much, Son, and we can't imagine our lives without you …

But we will carry on with the same pride and honor that you carried your-self, making the world a better place … One mind at a time …

Until I see you again, Dad

We will gladly accept the pain and anguish of losing our son, if it means he doesn't have to hurt anymore …

Evolution V 2.0 …

11.1.2015 … A time of wondrous anticipation for our trip to Peru … Education with a Destination … A chance to learn more about and experience the alpacas specifically, and camelids in general,in a completely different atmosphere, on a different part of the planet … The education we expected and the education that we were able to get in the Highlands, by observing and blessedly participating with these wonderful Peruvian animals … Getting to be one with the vicuna in Picotani ALONE was a lifetime of absolute education … and not just from a camelid breeder perspective … The Chaku was a wonderful opportunity to get up close to the vicuna in a way none of us anticipated.. Yes, running with the animals was absolutely magical in every way, but something else struck me … the people. The "coming together", if you will, of an entire community, unified for a common purpose, all within the realms of sacred tradition, given to them by the ones that preceded them … All in honoring the spirits that dwell here …

You could feel them, standing in a vast expanse of land, in the high plains of Peru … You could feel them in the Colca Valley at Corporaque at sunset … You could feel them in the streets of Arequipa, and the people we encountered all had that same sense of sacred, of tradition, of honoring and respecting those that came before us …

But the spirit that is there …

I thought I knew a lot about being a Catholic, and being "spiritual" from my upbringing … I knew a fair amount, chapter and verse, from Bible study long ago, but learning about the absolute FAITH and BELIEF the Peruvian people have, puts my education level at beginner … I learned so much more just by the interaction with people who have lived there all of their lives and are committed to their absolute faith absolutely … and the ones that were with us for more than an afternoon, were so unbelievably accommodating and generous with their time, their help, and their presence … Talks of the beauty of the land, of family, of experiences, of belief … All of the experiences we had in Peru have helped us with our herd and ways we can modify our program and our herd practices … But the entire experience gave me something more than an alpaca education … I experienced an awakening in spirit … a profoundly intense feeling of the connective energy between all spirits …

Almost like a closer look …

This awakening has been put to the most extreme test, I think, that a person should ever have to experience in any lifetime … While I have my faith, and my belief, the absolute pain of losing my son, at times, borders on unbearable … I look at some of the beauty from our trip in photos, and, for a moment, the pain lessens and the spirit is there …

A very brief moment …

I have learned a lot from my son, I have learned a lot about my son, and his belief in energy transference, means that while his physical presence is no longer here for us to see, his absolute presence is always here …

The lessons of the ones who have gone before us …

Spirit …

When your entire world comes crashing down around you, and physical and emotional interaction with ANYONE becomes practically unbearable, you start to look inward and rely on absolutely everything you believe in for answers, for comfort, for resolution … I believe that every living being has a spirit, soul, essence, whatever you wish to call it, that transcends this earthly vessel and becomes a part of everything else, ourselves included. …

We share earthly time with this spirit, and we connect, and over time, and shared experiences, that connection grows between the two spirits, forming an absolute bond, unbreakable and unique to each individual the spirit is connected with … My connection with Eric is such a bond … I believe that, in time, the connection we shared, and still share, will be reinforced once again … We are still reeling from the shock and mind numbing sadness of losing his physical presence, so "feeling" him around us is clouded by the darkness … It has been a blessing to be around so many individuals who have been touched and shared a connection with him, as we can see glimmers of him in them … We realize that once the initial kick to the chest has lessened, then, and only then, can we reinforce the electric spiritual connection that has been so strong for so long … There are little signs that his essence is still here … Although he had his own place in Castle Rock, he always considered this his home, and that holds true now … There are times late at night when I will get a faded whiff of his cologne, on the front porch a rustle in the leaves in the yard, the sound of the blackbirds taking wing in the darkness, the whisper of their wings as they take flight … The sound of the snowfall on the grass late on a Sunday afternoon … Bits and pieces, essences of the physical, reminders that the spirit is never really that far away …

The connection is still there …

Listening at the back door, I hear the sound of ice cracking in the trees as the breeze wafts gently through … Then the quiet …

Not a single sound …

I look about and I notice that everyone is huddled together in their respective pens, creating heat and security for everyone … The herd watches out for all within … It strikes me that these smaller circles form the outer edge of the larger circle, completed by the canine, feline and human souls who occupy this dwelling..

Respect is given to all, TO ALL, who visit here, human or otherwise …

We believe in the connections of those who have gone before us, and we feel their presence every now and again ... When it's quiet, when everyone is content, if you listen, really listen, you can hear remnants of whispers in the breeze ... Living in Eastern Colorado, away from the big cities and bright lights, affords an extraordinary amount of quiet time late at night ... The slight breeze helps to clear the fog inside my head, and helps me listen ... This is when I silently pray ... Pray for the strength to help those around me to make it through another day intact, pray for the clarity of mind, of spirit to keep focused on the tasks at hand, pray for the eventual opportunity to reunite with the ones that have gone before, pray that someday the pain of their physical absence will at least subside a little ...

As I pray though, I know in my heart of hearts, that I will willingly endure every last ounce of pain that I can, content in the fact that my son doesn't have to be in pain anymore ... I can live with that ...

My Truth ...

My truth is the one thing in this entire existence that is mine and mine alone, and has been since the day I was born.. Everything I have seen, done, felt, touched, tasted and experienced, has helped to mold me into the individual I am today, and, in turn, has also helped me spiritually, and taught me more about the connectivity of everything ... My truth is also molded, shaped, and formed by the individuals who stayed a spell, and either still reside here, or have moved on to other things ... everyone ... no matter how trivial the encounter ... everyone affects our truth ...

What you believe, how you believe, what is of "value" ... We argue about these things incessantly ...

My Truth is: I am going to believe what I believe, and you can go ahead and believe what you believe ... That's it ...

My Truth is there is beauty in everything ...

My Truth is that life and death are not the beginning and the end, rather 2 distinct transition points within the larger journey …

My Truth is that everyone, absolutely everyone we encounter can teach us something of value …

My Truth is that I learned to be a good father to my children, by having an absentee one myself …

My Truth is that ALL souls deserve respect and honor … The human race is not the be all, end all, but if we're not careful, we can certainly end it all …

My Truth, while spiritual, contains a dark side: a small room of sadness and regret … Regret for words unsaid, things undone … Profound, crippling sadness and sorrow about the loss of the human form, and the soul and personality contained therein …

The smile, the hug, the "I love you, Dad … "

I love you too, Son …

My Truth is that one, day, we will see each other again …

My Truth is who I am …

My Truth is me …

Namaste …

Writing during this time has proven to be very cathartic, and I am using this as an alternative to "therapy" … It is MY therapy, not in a group of people, but solitary … I have read so many wonderful emails and responses to these writings and I am humbled and grateful to the core … Several people have told me that writing about this experience takes "strength and courage" on my part …

I have no strength …

I have no courage …

All I have is love …

I want to tell the entire world about my son and the impact that he has had on me, my wife and daughter, and absolutely all of the ones he has touched in his life … I want the world to know about a fathers love for his only son, and the way that father is dealing, the way that father loves his son, unconditionally, without prejudice aforethought, with absolutely every fiber of my being. … Eric always hated the accolades, as he was humble, and believed in the power of the human spirit of the individual … That has helped me get out of bed in the morning, attempt to communicate verbally in every instance … There is only an extremely small group of people that I can talk to, albeit very, VERY briefly at this point … It has become easier to write, as I am alone, I don't have to have conversational linearity, and I can take my time to develop a thought, a passage, an idea … I can take my time to reveal with words the blessings that are bestowed on me, on us in this physical life … I want to share this through the written word, I need to write …

I can't speak, so I must write …

These days words are too often used to hurt and destroy … I want to use my words and his example to shift that to a more positive, a more blessed message; a message of hope and caring, healing and sharing..

I have no strength …

I have no courage …

All I have is love …

Love is all you need …

Namaste

Evolutionary Metamorphosis ...

As time marches on, and our son's passing gets further away, we can feel the transformation of self, and the changes that come along with it ...

For me, I can feel pieces of my previous self falling away like so many leaves falling from an aspen tree in the warm autumn breeze ... These pieces are slowly being replaced by the beginnings of a new self, a different individual, molded and shaped by the experiences of this journey through life ... The individual that I am becoming is foreign to me ... I am wading through all of the emotions and feelings of the last nine and a half weeks, still trying to organize my mind, and at least ATTEMPT to center myself ... Long hours, cold temperatures and the fact that its dark when I get home from work, have limited my time with the herd; with my girls ... I do spend time with the canine girls, and try to feel included in their pack ... They have been awkwardly accommodating, letting us in, however slightly ... As spring really starts to take a hold of the landscape, with more daylight available, it will be easier to be able to go and commune with them again ... Being surrounded by love and care has been very comforting to us, but, selfishly, I also need my herd ... I am anxious to go out to their pen for an extended period and be surrounded by them again ...

I really don't know what the future holds, as everything I am feeling, sensing, experiencing, is completely new on absolutely every level of my being ... I feel the pain of his loss every single day, and, every single day, I thank the Creator that I am still around ... The changes on the outside, the physical, have been somewhat noticeable to others ... The metamorphosis within, however, is enormous, and continually evolving, laying the groundwork for who I am to become ... For now, though, I must wait, I must feel, I must experience everything this journey brings, moving ever forward in the elusive quest for contentment and peace ...

Velocities ...

One thought entered my mind this morning, through the cranial fog of 5:30 ... It was a moment between my son and I, as we were getting ready to jump from a plane in our first, and only, solo skydive together. We had done a tandem jump on his birthday a year prior, with a photographer jumping with us to get the pics of the birthday boy's first reactions to flying ... Epic.

But I digress ...

We were in the plane, just about at altitude, 14,000 feet, when they opened the door. I remember the rush of cold air and adrenaline as I peered out the door to peek into the vastness before me. Eric asked me how high up it looked ... I told him, "It's not that we're high up, it's that we're far away ..."

"Dad, sit down ... You're starting to freak me out ..."

I sat down next to him, put my arm around his shoulder, reassuring him that, while it looked like a long way down, it was really just far away, and if that scared him, he should just look at the horizon; look at the curvature of the earth, and realize that you can see forever looking out ... look out, don't look down. Either way, the view is amazing. I think, when he saw the look on my face when I explained it to him, he was less nervous. I watched the muscles in his face relax, and his whole demeanor changed. He was looser and more ready to go. In that moment, that brief exchange between him and I, validated everything I needed to know about how to be a dad.

I told him that this was going to be the best feeling ever; a moment that we could relish for the rest of our lives. I decided to go first. You know, it's odd ... Before our tandem jump, I was the one that was a little apprehensive, as heights, up until that moment, scared the absolute shit out of me. This was different. I had a bit of knowledge from that one experience and an 8 hour training session under my belt, all fresh and vivid in my mind at the moment. But the moment itself ... I peered out the door again, this time, a bit longer to see a vision of the world few get to enjoy. The patchwork quilt of the earth before me. Farmland laid out in impossible shades of green and grey, the shadows of the clouds, now at our level, cast upon the land below adding to the shades. I looked out to the horizon as the handlers who would be with me for the first 30 seconds of the jump, went over last minute instruction and guidance. I fixed my gaze to the horizon, and fell into the vast. I looked down at the planet below me, marveling at the fact that I was now one with the birds; with the angels. I looked up again and saw the sky from the most uniquely beautiful perspective anyone could dream of.

I reached out and touched the face of God …

Blue …

As we watch events unfold in our world and in our lives, we see the emotional and psychological effects on our own personal beings, whether we choose to recognize them or not. We see people against each other, treating each other and the other inhabitants of the planet like garbage without a second thought as to their existence. These are individuals that do not have peace in their hearts and appear to be unwilling to educate themselves on the value and validity of other lives and other ideas. This is troublesome on so many levels. Our son, Eric, showed me a different view of the world and what it could be with the right mindset, and how to evolve to a better version of myself.

Blue is the color of the natural sky and sea. Blue is the color of peace and tranquility, and has shown cognitive properties of serenity and calm.

Blue4Eric was initially created as a remembrance for our son, and we have asked that people would wear blue, his favorite color, and now mine, to show remembrance for the extraordinary young man that he was and continues to be. The 2 days of the year that these "events" were to be held: May 24th, the day of his physical birth, and December 28th, the day of his departure from the physical world and his transformation to the spiritual realm. The spirit that carried him through his life while he was here, affected so many people around him, and helped those, who others wouldn't give a second thought.

His capacity for love, caring and sharing, in my opinion, is unmatched by anyone I have ever met in my existence. His light and energy have transcended what and who he was in this physical world, and his belief in the light and energy have made a positive impact on those of us blessed enough to be able to spend time in conversation with him.

So ...

This is now an evolution of purpose, an evolution of spirit, life and energy. The time has come to increase the peace, and up the ante on personal spirituality, energy and positivity. Blue4Eric is now a rally cry for our existence, our mindset and our future as a planet. We will incorporate his example on how to get through our day to day, through tolerance, acceptance, and love. One love for all. Period.

Unity in purpose, unity in resolve.

One Love ...

CHAPTER THREE

Water

Life ...

We give it, we take it, we decide it, we make it. Alpacas in our life have been a true blessing to us and our family. Has there been times of uncertainty..? Yes. Has there been times of hardship..? Absolutely.. But, at the end of the day, it has been completely worth it. We had a bit of trepidation when we first got in: not knowing anything about livestock, not knowing if we would be able to take care of these wonderful animals, not knowing the future ... That can be a deterrent to most of us, the whole 'not knowing' piece ... but we decided early on that we would not treat this as a deterrent; we decided that it would be a wonderful challenge, a business and personal decision that would enrich our lives and give purpose to our future ... Now I know that there are breeders out there that may or may not share this vision, but that's what we believe. I have seen all kinds of posts lately about breeders worrying about what other people say about how "The industry is in a decline ... " We believe just the opposite. We feel that with the proper business plan and positive outlook about alpacas, we can make this entire industry sustainable and, in the end, quite profitable. We choose to not listen to the naysayers and continue to follow our optimism; the same optimism that led us to purchase our herd in the first place. Do we question some of these "Debbie Downers"..? Yes. But we have seen "work arounds".. A different way to do things, "thinking outside the pen" if you will ... Those who are not happy in their own lives, trash the happy ones to make themselves feel better ... Not us.. We are in this for the long haul. Forge ahead and follow what you believe.. Don't be blind to the negativity; embrace the positivity, and know that what you are doing is for the good of all. And that really what it's all about, isn't it..?

Who out there is tired of both all of the bad news every night as well as the continuing political ads that have enveloped every last bit of our media and, by extension, our consciousness these days..? Terrorism, murder, sadness EVERYWHERE. ... And it doesn't matter whether its TV, radio or the internet.. When it all becomes too much, which, is like at 8:30 in the morning, I turn off all of the technology, and head out to the pens.. I would much rather deal with alpaca poo than the monumental amount of people poo that just seems to happen every day.. There is no sadness out there. Just peacefulness and tranquility … And isn't that really better for the mind, body and soul..? Every single day I can spend even a little time with the alpacas, they help to keep my mind in check, my body healthy and my soul at peace … If you are ready for a change in the way that you look at life and how you are living, you, too should become one with the herd …

As alpaca breeders we have experienced the good and the bad, the happy and the sad, and we are blessed.. We feel that there is value to all of it. As we near the end of 2014, we reflect on the past year and all of the things we have experienced the last year and our 8 years in the industry …

Are we where we want to be..? Not yet..

Are we successful..? I believe so, yes..

Our success is not measured by the amount of money in our bank account, or by the number of banners on the wall.. Success, for us, is our animals are happy, healthy and we have learned so many valuable lessons in our time with the alpacas.. We have received advice from many breeders, and we value everyone's opinion on our farm and our industry. We believe that there is a tremendous learning experience with all of it; positive and negative. We try to keep our minds open to absolutely everything we see, hear and read … It all helps us to become better as alpaca breeders and as individuals … We also have learned from our animals and their reactions to different things on the farm, as well as in the pens at the show. We are not so knowledgeable that we can't stop learning from everyone and all of their experiences as well; from the breeder that has been in the industry for 25 years as well as the new breeder who has just brought their animals home … All of this has value to us … We believe that we need to get past the limits of who we are and what we know, and open ourselves to experience and understanding.

Because when we do that — when we kill our ego — it actually helps us to achieve the highest and best expression of who we are, and who we were made to be.

A Revelation …

I started my day today, just like I do every day. Cop of coffee, feed the dogs, feed the cats, brush my teeth, get dressed and go outside to do chores. Rather innocuous really. Today was clean the pens day, so I started on that first thing. As I was cleaning the pens, I noticed the dogs playing in the back 2 and a half, like they do every day. Then it hit me. Here we have all of these animals, llamas, alpacas, dogs and cats, but the one group's members that are so radically different, are the dogs. Sable, a German Shepherd; Phoebe, a Akbosh/Pyrenees mix; Maddie, a black lab, and Taima, a Rottweiler/Jack Russell mix. Yet, as different as these 4 are, they play together, eat together, sleep together, and, form the team that protects the property … together. They watch out for one another, and keep each other in check. Always. I started to think about how each of them was so radically different, but still managed to stay together as a team; each from a different place when they were born, each with their own strengths and weaknesses, yet managing to operate as a team. Are there conflicts..? Of course there are, but they are resolved quickly, and without bloodshed. They work it out.

Humans, on the other hand, seem to want to categorize absolutely everything, creating perceived, and in some cases, real separation. Not just with animals, but with each other.

Black/White/Brown

American/Afghani/Russian

Democrat/Republican

Christian/Muslim/Atheist

Straight/Gay/Trans

Rich/Poor

Humans do this to create groups, and I really don't understand that. We are all human, what difference does it make..? These types of attitudes divide us exponentially, at a time when we should really come together for the good of all humanity. The people in power are the ones that perpetuate the fear and hate, and that needs to stop. How can we call these people our "leaders" when all they are interested in, is their own financial security? I see on the news, and out in the world, people use these categories to belittle, and demean each other, simply because of a label that has been put on them. I have gay friends, and black friends. I have Christian friends and Muslim friends, but I don't categorize them like that. They are just my friends. I used to have Democrat and Republican friends, but they were so into trying to prove the other party wrong, and vilifying themselves as right, that I just didn't have time for that nonsense.

Society is so quick to put labels on everyone these days, that people can't just be people anymore. They have to be a White American, or a Black Muslim, or whatever. We have developed a hatred for groups of people, simply because of what they believe, or where they are from, and I think that sucks.

How the FUCK are we going to learn anything if we hate what's different..? I have decided, in my life, to take my son's example and base a person on the type of person that they are, not their nationality, or religion, or skin color.

Life is far too short to limit who you can learn something from.

Think I'll be like the dogs …

Animal lives matter …

One of the many things that are part of my ever-evolving core belief system, is the fact that animal lives matter … Not just the ones that cohabitate with us, here on this farm, and, frankly, wherever we go, but the ones that occasionally visit these 4 fence lines. As an inhabitant of this planet, I feel that it is my honor, my duty, and my blessing to be able to witness nature here, in the 4-legged form, as well as the winged and the insect forms as well. All forms of life are respected and honored for exactly the being and the spirit that they represent. As I have grown older and grown away from the suburbia mentality that gripped my adolescent mind, I have come to see the animal form as more sacred, more primal, more pure. I have grown weary of all the expectations and limits that the human animals place on me and the ones I love, in the everyday corporate milieu … In the realm of the natural, there are only a few expectations, and those come from the primal instinct: shelter, safety, and sustenance. And these are gladly given, no questions asked, no notice needed. These are the life blessings that I enjoy: to be a caretaker to these beings, as they provide me with something most human beings on this planet could never provide; unquestioning, unwavering loyalty, love and trust. These I would never betray, not even in the most heinous of circumstances. These are the ones that have, and continue to trust that I, and we, will take care of them, love them, and make sure of their health, safety and well-being. In the world we live in, where the majority of the human population is in it for their own interests and materialism, my tranquility and peace lie within the animal population. The lessons that these beings provide me, far outweighs any book knowledge I have gained in the last 50+ years of my life. I have learned the primal ceremonies of life and of death, since we have been able to have these wonderful animals in our lives, be it canine, feline or camelid. I have watched the interaction of all these species within these premises, and sat in wonder as they try to figure out what each other's part in the herd order shall become. They interact more out of curiosity, than out of fear or retribution; a timid respect for each other's existence. That isn't to say that there hasn't been the odd confrontation, establishing boundaries and territory. There has, but once that territory has been established, it is respected. As one of 3 human animals within this plot of land, all territories established are respected, and treaded upon lightly, to mitigate any sense of human entitlement, out of respect for the individual animal occupants within. That is the one thing that has been established, for the most part here; a respect for personal and individual space, a place to feel safe and secure from the ravages of the outside world. I have seen what the human animal does to the beings in their care, and it is appalling. The purity of animal life seemingly has no sacred space in some human lives. Neglect, abuse, and downright torture of some animals on the planet is incorrigible, so much so, that it is my opinion, that, if someone is caught being inhumane to an animal, they should be treated the exact same way. People who engage in dog fighting, trophy hunting and the like, just for the mere fun of killing, should be condemned to isolation within our society, chained to a wall and forgotten about. That is how passionate I am about honoring and respecting the brethren of other species here, on this planet.

Lines …

Yesterday as I was dragging the girls front pasture, I was looking at the ground, making sure that I was getting all the areas turned up before we got some much needed moisture, here on the farm. Weather this winter has been extremely dry in Colorado, so the ground was a little more than a little parched and hardened, so it took a couple of passes to actually make a difference. As I kept going, and the tines on the harrow rake kept getting deeper into the barren soil, I started to see patterns emerge. The darkness of the soil underneath started to peak out amongst the lines I was raking, making linear patterns of earth. A life size Zen garden, if you will. The impaction of the ground was helped along by the female alpacas and their babies running, cushing and playing on it for the better part of the last year. Matted down by the constant traffic of alpaca and llama feet, the plants under the surface didn't have a chance to peek out and at least attempt, to grow.

As I started, I went in one general direction, making the ground look like the musical staff of a blank sheet of music. Second pass, same direction, only this time a bit deeper, and as I went through, I noticed rocks under the surface were starting to appear, looking like notes on the sheet of music. I also noticed the alpacas were on the fence line, in a perfect straight line, looking at me like I was tearing their world apart. I actually stopped what I was doing at this point and explained to them, that what I was doing was for their benefit: creating softer ground for them to relax, as well as helping the plants underneath the soil come up for them to graze on later in the spring. And they were not very amused, but they seemed to understand.

I kept dragging the pasture, back and forth, different directions, with dust blowing everywhere. When I finished, I noticed something other than the patterns I had noticed before, as I was inspecting my work. Lines, a lot of lines, intersecting in every direction, but all connected. There isn't a single line that stands alone. The image stayed with me as I went to bed last night.

Upon waking this morning, I had a very stark image in my head, and immediately wrote it down so as not to forget it. The image was of every human, and every being on the planet, transmitting their own individual frequency out to the world, not unlike the myriad of cell phone and communication towers that inhabit the landscape. These are used to amplify the reception and transmission of signals, so that, at least electronically, we are connected. Each and every being on the planet emits a frequency, and those who choose to receive the signal are drawn to each other.

Like frequencies attract like frequencies. The ebb and flow of life, the events and circumstances that shape us, modify the frequencies we accept and gravitate towards, and in turn, the people who drift in and out of our lives. And the frequencies we transmit and receive are ever changing, but the ones that we gravitate towards in shared life experiences, tend to be the ones who stay with us.

Family …

With the holidays upon us, we tend to concentrate on our loved ones a little more, celebrating each other and spending a little more time together … Related or not, we have people in our lives that we consider "family" … On our farm, we firmly believe that all of our animals are part of our family … While we are in the business of selling alpacas and alpaca related products, we believe that all of our animals are more of a community than a commodity … Are we in this business for the "business" aspect..? Absolutely … We market and sell our animals just like all of the other farms out there, but our philosophy is based more on how the individual alpaca IS, not how much money they can make for us … We make sure that they are going to farms and individuals who will take care of them much in the manner that we do ... We try to make decisions for our animals that are in the best interest and welfare of the animal. That's not to say we are going to spend an exorbitant amount of money on an animal that cannot be saved ... We look at the individual situation and make the reasonable decision based on all factors of that situation..

Is it sometimes sad..? Of course it is ... But that's the nature of nature ...

We have seen our herd exhibit all of the facets and feelings that human families exhibit, but theirs is more real; more profound.. We laugh, they pronk ... We get sad, they get subdued ... We argue, they argue.. We mourn, they mourn ... We, as humans, tend to give human emotions and traits to our animals, and, in a way, I think that lessens these for them ... Theirs is more primal, rooted in instinct and herd behavior ... All animals are infinitely more majestic and pure than we, as humans, could ever HOPE to be.. And as humans, it's important to understand all of that for what it is.. No objectivity, just survival, and understanding our place within the herd. ... Working for the betterment and the survival of the herd; of the family ... Once we take the time to actually see and try to understand them, then maybe, just maybe, we can try to understand each other a little better ...

Resolutions ...

With the Holiday Season winding down, it's acknowledged that we have to start thinking about getting back into the everyday swing of things again ... New Years Eve is in a couple of days and we are in the process of trying to figure out what we would like to do or improve ourselves going forward into 2015 ... Lose some weight, be more forgiving, take more time with others, and quitting smoking all seem to be right at the top of everyone's list in some form or another ... I, and by extension, we, resolve to inform as many people as possible about all of the joy and satisfaction we have experienced in our time with our alpacas here on the farm ... We believe strongly that the alpacas have provided us with so much more than the monetary aspect ... We have also learned a great many things from them as well, and we have been able to transform that knowledge into our everyday lives ... When we introduce the herd to others [friends, family, etc ...] that have never been around them, you can see the joy and wonderment in their eyes ... Even the most jaded horsemen in our neighborhood, would look at them and inquire about absolutely everything the alpaca has to offer us and our farm ... Children get that "Christmas morning" look on their faces when the see the babies playing in the front pasture ... It also helps that our girls are very inquisitive about the little ones that come to visit, sniffing them and looking for pellets in their pockets whenever they come into the pen ... Even now as the snow and cold have enveloped the countryside, people still brave the cold weather, bundle up, and come hang out with the alpacas ... You can see the true meaning of peace and tranquility in our visitors souls when they spend time with the animals ... This truly has been the best investment and greatest blessing that we, as regular people, could EVER have imagined ... We control our own assets and income, and the large financial markets have no "say-so" over how much our earnings will be ... We have realized that the alpacas truly are "live stock", and the financial, emotional and spiritual gains are practically endless ... Resolve to make everything about your life better ... It is possible ...

An Appreciation ... .

Our journey with the alpacas started in 2007, and we have experienced all kinds of things in our time with them. ... We acquired our herd while we still lived in a neighborhood, boarding our animals at the farm we bought our starter herd from ... Since then, we have experienced the good, the bad, and our own small tragedies.. There have been lessons in all of it, and we are grateful. I am grateful for things that I never would have thought possible 25 years ago.. I am grateful for my wife, for "pushing the issue" all those years ago ... It is because of her that we have alpacas to begin with, and the happiness that the alpacas provide has been immeasurable.. I am grateful for the many breeders who have taken their time and effort to show us many different ways to raise and care for alpacas, expanding our knowledge for these wonderful animals ... I am eternally grateful for the breeder friends we have made in our time with the alpacas; the ones that have been there since the very beginning [this means you, ShareBear ...] I am grateful for the people who have asked a million questions about the alpacas, and the interest they have shown towards our animals ... I am grateful for all of the help we received from our neighbors in Elizabeth when we first moved here; helping with the fencing, shelters and snow removal when that was needed ... I am grateful to the breeders from other states that have extended courtesies to us when we were "on the road" at their home state shows ... You know who you are ... I am grateful for all of the animals that have ever spent time in our little slice of Heaven.. Because of all of them we have increased our knowledge as well as our consciousness ... They have showed us an appreciation for nature that living in a neighborhood could not provide ... I am grateful for the people and animals in our lives that have gone before us, for their love, trust and companionship.. They are remembered and revered for the lessons have so generously given to us ... Lastly, I am very grateful for all of you, the ones who read the rantings presented here, and have read and "liked" them on Facebook, the ones who comment and share the words in the groups and our page.. You have also provided a much needed education and also a forum for me and us to "bounce" things off of ... My, and our, appreciation for all of you is boundless and endless ...

Time ...

We give time, take time, have time, make time. ... Time is money, time is fleeting, time is all we have really ... And we never have enough of it. The last few days of the year are fleeting by, barreling into the next, and a new beginning ... Hope springs eternal with a new year upon us, all of us hoping that the new year will be better than the last one ... There will be some new hello's, a few will say goodbye, and we will learn even more about ourselves and those around us ... That's the way it goes ... Time marches on and we march with it ... Time can also be an investment into how we act/react towards all of the situations that come our way going forward ... If we vow and resolve to make ourselves better in the new year, then we must stick to it ... And I'm not talking about the "stop smoking, lose weight" resolutions ... The weight we really need to lose is above the neck, not below it ... The weight of hate, of acrimony, of misunderstanding and anger ... That is all dead weight that drags us all down, that slows the process of growth ... I mean, think of the time that was spent this past year worrying about what others did, said, meant, and how this affected us in a negative way ... That same time and energy could be used more constructively, creating the positivity for our own existences ... Don't allow others to live in your head, rent free ... That's how we choose to live ... We only worry about the things that are under our control ... Take time to make time to help and encourage others be the best they can be ... Spread the light.. ...

A joyous New Year to you all, and may you be blessed as we go into the next ...

There can be only one ...

You cant have "Unique" without U ... You are the only you there is ...

While I was doing chores this afternoon, I was looking at all of our animals, eating hay and humming, and I was struck by something. No two are the same ... Just like us people ... No two are the same ... Even if we have the same herdsire and dam, mom and dad, we are all different, and that's kinda cool, isn't it..? We all have different likes, different views and opinions, different tastes and different ideas ... We, as humans, have roughly the same biological makeup, but each one of us are as individual as our own fingerprints ... Sure, we may all like the same music, the same sports teams, the same color alpacas as others, but we all have our own daily rituals, dreams, goals and aspirations ... Something that I may like, you could hate, and vice versa, but that makes neither of us superior or inferior to each other; it just makes us different; unique ... If we can respect the uniqueness that we each have, then we can learn from these differences and grow as individuals and as a part of the larger herd ... I will be me and you can be you, ok..? That's all I ask of any one person, animal, entity, whatever ... Don't be afraid to disagree with something if you genuinely don't agree with them; and, on the flipside, don't attack

64

someone for disagreeing with you ... Embrace their differences instead of criticizing them ... That's why we love every single one of our alpacas ... Each one has a different look, personality, and way they go through their day ... Are some more of a pain in the ass then others..? Sure, but we don't love them any less for that ... It's who they are, its who they want to be ... The Creator made them that way, each their own individual, and who are we to disagree with that..? Same with people.. That same Creator made us each different and unique, with different minds, different bodies, and different gifts ... We try to embrace the differences and learn and grow from each and every one we come in contact with, be it face to face, on the phone or electronically ... Tolerance isn't inborn into our systems, but each day we can try and grow enough to learn from each other and love each other for who we are, not by who we want each other to be ... Love yourself, be tolerant of yourself, and you will be surprised at how easy the rest falls into place ..

You be you and I'll be me ...

A new dawn, a new day ...

First of all, Happy New Year to all of my, and our, friends.. Today is the beginning of another chapter in our lives ... A clean slate, a blank page, a new 365 day episode in the story of our existence ... Hope is not a campaign slogan for a politician to use as a selling tool, it is a state of mind for us to believe that everything will be alright ... Woke up this morning to the sun coming up, lighting the way and the world as we enter 2015 ... A hopeful sign, and, as it was quiet, a peaceful sign ... All the animals were cushed in their respective pens, eating hay and humming ... Content with their existence, relaxed and basking in the glow of a new day ... We have hope for the new episode in our lives, and pray for the good in everyone ... We have 8 crias due this year, 8 potential color champions, 8 brand new additions to our wonderful herd, and we are filled with hope and expectation that these "kids" will all be happy, healthy and full of the same wonder and spirit that this day provides us ... I look at the beginning of a new year like skydiving ... You get to altitude, and they make the announcement ...

New Years Eve is the door opening, and you allow yourself a glimpse into what you are about to embark upon … You stand in the doorway, looking out … New Years Day … Then you jump, headlong into the expanse, not knowing how its all going to play out … There's a million different scenarios that could play out, and you are there, weightless, taking in the view, the wonder of a 3 year old at Christmas in your eyes and your heart.. It is all over way to quickly, and you rely on what you have been taught to get you to the ground safely … You land at the end, and instinctively look up, like you just had a small conversation with God … That's how I like to look at the New Year … So much can and will happen, and not always under our control, but if we embrace all of the experiences to come and look at each of them objectively, we can learn from all of them and grow … There are no problems, only ways to learn and improve who we are as individuals and as members of the herd …

We all have something that we believe in … Maybe even several things … Belief in a higher power, belief in our loved ones, belief in our principles, belief in a million other things … I think as humans, to be able to get through everyday life, we really need something or someone to believe in … My day gets exponentially better when I realize that my belief in my Creator and my herd is undying and perpetual … My herd includes ALL of the animals that reside here, my kids, my brother and, most importantly, my wife Rael Reddick … She has believed in me for over 20 years now, and I know how hard I am to live with and deal with on a daily basis … She came into my life at a point when I really didn't believe in myself very much … I was on a path of self destruction that I didn't see any way out of, and she pulled me from the precipice … For that, I am eternally grateful … She has also "made my mind right", introducing me to an alternative to the way I was thinking back then … She gave me a very beautiful introduction to the ways of nature and the importance of any and all animals in our existence, and, for that, I am also grateful … Because of her, we are a fully functioning alpaca farm … Because of her, we live in the country … Because of her, I am alive to be able to raise the kids and the alpacas in an absolutely beautiful, tranquil atmosphere … It's this belief in the power of nature and the beauty of animal life that has renewed my faith in the power of the Creator …

I was raised in the Catholic church, by my mothers grace and had a very well rounded education about what my religious beliefs are founded in to this day.. Then, I became a young adult who "knew better", and didn't think that I needed faith in my life anymore.. You know, except when I needed something, or needed to get out of trouble ... THATS when I would pray and ask God to help me out with some assistance ... Now that I am older, I have adjusted that thinking exponentially to where I am today ... With the aforementioned assistance from the love of my life ... I have come to believe that everything happens in our lives for a reason ... Life, death, good times and bad, it all happens for a reason.. And I believe that the reason is to make us more "well versed" in the things that we need to know and experience in this existence to help us in the next ... Alpacas happened in our lives, I believe, to teach us tolerance and the need to care for another than our particular species; to experience something vastly different than the cookie cutter neighborhood that I was raised in and lived in until I was 41 years old ... Until our alpacas became a part of my consciousness, the neighborhood was all I knew.. Going to that first alpaca show, because of Rael, has completely changed and altered what and how I believe in absolutely everything in my existence; physical, emotional, psychological and especially spiritual ... I believe in the power of the herd and the way of life we have chosen ... And for these, I believe that we are truly, TRULY blessed ...

We all make mistakes.. I KNOW I have made my share ... Maybe more than my share.. But, I am only human.. And humans make mistakes.. The thing is, is that we can correct these and try to do better the next time around, learning and growing from them ... It's very important that we DO learn from them and teach others about the mis-steps that we make, so that they, and we can do well in this life ... As a society I believe it is crucial to make the decisions that not only benefit ourselves but others as well.. Have we made mistakes with our herd..? You bet.. I think we all do, but we learn from these and, hopefully we, and the herd all benefit from it ... We are very fortunate, at our farm, that the errors we have made have not cost any animals their lives ... Knock on wood, the herd will continue to prosper under our care, and not have any of them suffering because of it ... It is inherently up to us to make sure our herd is safe from harm, fed and cared for, and make sure their existence is as carefree; helping them thrive and prosper in their human made environment ... The herd is free to move about within their pen and their front pasture as they please, unencumbered by restraint ... Free to be what they want to be, to do what they want, separated by gender, so as not to cause each other harm and undue stress.. When we started raising alpacas, we visited numerous farms and learned from them; asking the questions that we felt were imperative for the success, safety and health of our herd.. We asked what they would do differently if they were just starting their herd, and every single one of them was candid and honest ... That is one of the things that we like about raising alpacas; that many other breeders are open and honest with their suggestions, and very friendly to boot ... We have also met breeders who happen to be judges in the industry and asked them questions while we were at their farms as well, and they were no less candid, honest and friendly ... You can tell the type of person you are dealing with by how they care for their animals ... The love and caring shines through when you visit their farm ... Even in a neighborhood setting, how people care for their animals is a direct reflection on who they are as a person; as a human being ... I have seen stories and posts on Facebook about individuals who abuse and even kill animals for sport, for fun, for the hell of it, because they think it makes them a bigger person, or because it's funny ... Got news for you who do this; it's not fun, it's not funny, and it sure as HELL doesn't make you a bigger person ... It makes you soulless and evil.. The animals, and people for that matter, who you have in your charge, trust that you are going to do right by them, to take care of them, to nurture and love them for the rest of their existence on this planet ... We have a female on this farm that is a rescue animal; she was mistreated and abused to the point of mistrust for EVERYONE, but we took her in anyway ... Through many months of being spit at, stomped, and kicked, we did everything to care for and try to "rehabilitate" her ... Not by physical violence, but by caring for her, feeding her and loving her for what she brings to our herd ... And slowly, surely, she has come to trust Rael and I, to the point of being able to hug here and letting her know that she can trust us by how she is treated ... That's what being human means to me; treat others, ALL others, as you would have them treat you ... Does it always work..? No, unfortunately ... But I believe that you will never know unless you try ...

Make a difference by making the effort ...

Sometimes there is nothing like going out, after evening chores are done and just sitting in the pen with the girls and just ... listening ... Finding a spot on the ground, near the hay where they all are and just listening to the calm, tranquil sound of a day turning to evening ... The alpacas all have their hay, and they are all starting to cush in front of their own flake, with the sound of them eating; cooing and humming all the while ... I like to do that in the dead of winter as well, taking a few extra minutes inside the shelter where all of the girls have gathered, out of the snow and cold that's happening just outside their shelter, to enjoy their late afternoon repast ... Doing nothing but sitting on the ground and observing; enjoying every single second I have to spend with them ... this is my time, the time I take, however long I need, to connect, to become a small part of their world, their existence, if only for a short while.. These are the times that I feel like a part of the herd ... I look nothing like them, but they are ok with my being there among them ... Sometimes they notice my presence, but more often than not, they just go about their feast, seemingly oblivious to my human intrusion. I like to think that they are ok with me being there among them ... Accepted as one of them, a member of the exclusivity of the herd ... It is these times that I feel less as an individual and a part of everything else that the Creator has bestowed around me ... These are the times when the intrusiveness of being a human being, bogged down with the responsibility of all things adult, of all the stresses of the everyday, just drift away and I am with them; the herd that we so lovingly care for and observe, mostly from afar.. These are the times when my heart fills with joy and love for these beings of another species, that they would even THINK to include me in their circle is enormously humbling, as I have seen what human beings are capable of ... These are the moments of clarity that envelope me, when I feel closest to my Creator and I can cleanse my soul and become part of the ancestral, primal and tribal ONE ... One Earth, one life, intertwined with everything else, letting go of the ego that so often traps us and holds us down ... These are the moments when I stop being a Human Being, and become a Human Doing, existing within the life cho- sen for me, doing the needful to become serene and tranquil, one breath, one heartbeat, one existence among the herd ... I have found my Nirvana, my Namaste, my Holy Spirit, my meaning … That is the meaning of life; to enjoy each other and learn by coexisting with one another, in harmony with all that is around you, no matter how large, no matter how small … Every living being needs to have a place where they feel safe, where they feel that they belong and, to some extent, where they feel loved … Some call that home, some call it church or synagogue, some may even call it their happy place … It is the one place on the planet where the calmness and serenity can shut out the troubles, trials and tribulations of an otherwise savage world … Outside is where they don't understand you, where they really don't care about what happens as you go about your day, your life … But in here. … In here is where the warmth caring and compassion of the souls and lives around you, care … No matter what goes on "out there", we always have "in here".. Its where we have each other, where those who understand us, and are of similar mindsets, reside … the herd is here; the ones who are happy to see you in the morning, afternoon and evening … The ones who will listen to your troubles and sit with you in silence, knowing, somehow, that their mere presence makes it all better … And it does … There's a comfort and serenity there … And it doesn't even have to be a building or a specific place on the map.. It can be as simple as being with and within members of your own herd … On the road at a show, in the trailer, getting ready to embark upon another fantastic adventure, sitting in the pen, listening to the hums and coos coming from the four legged friends who happen to dwell there … YOUR herd, YOUR place, YOUR peace … All of the members of the herd are integral in making the whole of our sanity a very real and tangible thing … Wherever, whenever, however you feel safe and accepted for all you are and all you will become, with those who matter, it doesn't matter who … that's where we want to be; where we need to be; that's where our happiness and security lies … Its where we achieve our greatest accomplishments, and we are comforted in our greatest tragedies, by the ones who mean the most, and care the most … Where our souls are at peace and we feel like we belong; where we are one with everything … I believe this where the Creator resides; within … I can always handle "doing" within, I can never handle "doing" without …

Tribal …

Family, village, herd, tribe, community …

I was raised by both of my parents, but I was taught to be the man I am today by my mother … It is from her that I have learned the essence of all of my spiritual values that I eschew to this day … It is also from her that I learned of my physical lineage; where I come from … I learned that my father's side was basically English, Irish and Welsh, but on her side was the Irish and "Indian", if you will pardon the expression … I prefer the term "Native" … That is the part of my heritage that I most identify with; the part I have studied the most about in my life … From a young age, I discovered that I had a real problem with the way all of my father's European ancestors and some of my mother's treated the Native peoples on this continent … It was the Northeastern tribes I wanted to know about, as that is where my ancestors dwelled … With that knowledge, I was able to immerse myself in all of the tribes of the United States, as well as the First Nation people of Canada … Practices, beliefs, customs, stories, it all fascinated me … There really was nothing too concrete in the American History books at school, aside from the chapter and verse that school children were force fed at that particular time … So I asked my mother to enlighten me on the ways of the Iroquois, and the nature of nature … Learning of the ways of the ancestors gave me a light into my being that was "kinda" there, but only through what I had learned from the matriarch of my family at the time … Since then, through many Gatherings of Native people I have learned an expanded appreciation for Mother Earth and all living things and how we are all related.. I have communed with our animals, and listened as I never would have thought possible 30 years ago … My mind has exploded with all of the new and important things that raising alpacas, and living in wide open spaces, has brought to my heart and my consciousness … In the process I have learned the importance of the herd, of the community of all living things … The connection that we have with each other, with all of the inhabitants of this planet … That is what I want to take from this life; there are really no unimportant lives … All lives have something to teach all of us … Be it positive lessons, or the random negative experience, there is something to learn from all of it … And, if we are lucky, we are able to learn a little something about our own individual selves … One herd, one community, making a positive difference to change the world … One life at a time …

Shepherd …

As an alpaca breeder, I, personally, have never really been really comfortable with the word "owner" … I have always believed that one life does not simply "own" another life … I like to think of us as "caretakers" … We are caretakers for our family, and in my eyes at least, all of the animals on this property are members of our family; our herd, if you will … We do everything within our power to make sure that they are all healthy, well fed and well taken care of … Rael and I like to joke that we have 2 kids, and 33 children … because, in a manner of speaking, they ARE our children … We are there when they are born and we watch with parental pride as they grow, acclimate to their relevance within the herd and become their own, individual adult being … We marvel at what they learn and see for the first time much in the same way we do with our own human children; we "celebrate" their firsts and watch their personalities develop into their adulthood splendor … They are there for us when we need a break from the everyday "people herd" outside these fencelines, and genuinely seem to understand that need … they are there to sit with us, and listen to us prattle on about our daily grievances with humanity … Or they just sit with us and hum. … that's how I like to decompress, just listening to the hum and the soft munching of hay … Watching the babies pronk all over the front pasture in the late spring/early summer is absolutely the best activity to enjoy when the sun is setting … Sitting in the back pasture when we let the girls out on the property with their young ones is like a day at the park, watching the children play tag and finding all of the flowers and sights and smells that this "place out back" has to offer them … Its uplifting to see the babies who meet their father (provided they are on this property) for the first time … Its almost as though the herdsire will recognize their progeny, and for the briefest of moments, they become tender and recognize that this little one is theirs …

We have met breeders who look at their alpacas as a commodity, and, I guess to some extent with all of us, they are ... We, however, tend to look at their value as far more than monetary.. Their value to us lasts a whole lot longer than any amount of money ever could ... the peace of mind and lessons they teach us is priceless ... They are our community ... and we take care of our community ... It takes a herd ...

Rebirth ...

With Ash Wednesday just past and the beginning of the Easter season upon us, we realize, no matter what the weather may have in store, that Spring is just around the corner ... In Colorado, we haven't seen the extreme weather that has managed to grip a large part of the nation lately, but, even here, we see signs of the new season starting to unearth itself all around us ... little sprigs of green in the pastures, trees starting to begin the process of budding out, the birds are starting to become more plentiful within the landscape ... Even the sun, when we see it, seems to be a bit warmer on our faces ... Even the pregnant girls on our farm are starting to get round and ready for the beauty of cria birth; something we look forward to every year ... The seasonal cycle renews again and we are blessed to be able to enjoy this new cycle every year ... We have noticed that the cold and darkness of Winter has taken its toll on all living things, especially this year, making humans and animals alike a little more hot tempered, a little more antagonistic, and a little less caring about anything except their own circumstances ... We have, in previous Winters, been faced with the same extreme weather and cold, and Spring always managed to come with new life and new mindset.. It can be difficult, with these conditions, at times to remain positive and actually believe that the warmth and beauty of Spring will show its sunny face again ... But we persevere, fighting through the negativity, ever hopeful, ever vigilant that this year, this day, this Spring will come, and with it, the promise of all of the beauty, warmth and light that the new season provides all of us ... The soul can finally be replenished and the positivity can grow again, making all of the cold and dark disappear for another season ... We believe that this time of year is crucial to our physical, mental and especially spiritual well being and functionality, in that, we can recharge our "batteries" and grow, prosper and move ever forward, making our lives and existences a better place, and, by extension, the lives and souls around us as well; better, brighter, and happier ... These are the thoughts and feelings that get us through the dark and cold of Winter: Its a new dawn, its a new day, its a new life ... and I'm feelin' good ...

In our life, we celebrate new life and celebrate those lives that have mattered most to us after they depart this mortal coil. When I was younger, I always had a hard time with death and dying, and the perceived "finality" of the whole thing ... As a child, I was always sheltered from that side of life; if we had a dog that needed to be put down, Mom and/or Dad would have us say goodbye, and take them to the vet.. We never really knew what happened, other than our dog was no longer there ... As I grew older, and was emotionally able to handle it more, I got to go to the vet with them and say my goodbyes there in the vets office, still not too sure what was going on behind the big white door ... Death was fairly antiseptic in our house; my mother didn't want to talk about it, and Dad just flat out refused to discuss it; end of story ... It wasn't until I was out on my own and able to determine what I could and could not see for myself, that I began to really understand what the 'end of life' entailed ... As an adult, I have seen life ebb away slowly with my Mother, as she lost her battle with cancer; I have seen life extinguished in the blink of an eye, never evil or with malice aforethought, but death nonetheless ... It still always amazes me, no matter what time of day that it is, when a life ends, the silence is so deafening ... Its like the world around you has stopped everything to pay small tribute to the being going on to the next existence ... To the next adventure ... We look at the birth of all living things as a miraculous and beautiful experience, and there is so much joy surrounding this blessed event ... When someone crosses from this life to the next, more often than not, it is monumentally sad and somber ... I feel, that in the right context, this event can be no less beautiful ... We witness the transition from physical life to the other side; what we cannot see from this vantage point ... I have felt the spirit in the room and the pasture.. And, in one instance, I have seen, and see everyday, the return of our beautiful Ginger ... I believe that the spirits are here with us everyday, but there is

74

just something about a certain cria on the property ... His mannerisms, his look, his EVERYTHING is Ginger ... I have tried to discount it in my own head, but then something he does, or a look,. ... That's Ginger. ... I believe in the presence of spirits and I believe that, in some capacity, they will always be here for us, with us ... But when the physical manifestation of a departed soul starts to show within the herd.. ... I don't question it anymore, I just enjoy the memory of our Ginger, and spending time with the cria that also has my heart. ... and my soul ...

Find that inner music; that inner harmony that keeps you going in your day to day ... Its in there. ... everyone has their own rhythm, their own melody, their own harmony. ... Most days its muted by the everyday obligations of the outside life we have chosen for ourselves ... Its there. ... You have to remove yourself from all of the clutter and put yourself in a quiet place. ... late nights and really early mornings, I have found, are generally the optimum time for spiritual decompression ... When you're outside, and the only sound you hear is the sound of the animals munching on hay and stirring for the day, you can almost hear the heartbeat of the planet ... It's the same at three o'clock in the morning ... Watching the moon rise, and listening to the birds start their day, sparse at first but growing in volume and intensity as the first rays of the new day start to show themselves ... The music of the planet. ... in tune with the rhythm of yourself..

Outside the fence ...

In my day to day, I come in contact with all kinds of different people from different backgrounds, different heritages and different countries ... And, sadly, the majority of them are all about how much money they make, what they own, who they know, and what they are doing ... I have discovered that the majority of these people are running about their lives, oblivious to the rest of the world around them ... they are condescending about those of us who have chosen the country life and the peace and space it offers ... They try to convince me that they have it made; a house in the exclusive neighborhood, the newest car and they make some ungodly amount of money working in, what amounts to, a concrete bunker, ordering others to do their bidding ... I used to accept this as normal in society today, but now ...

When I was laid off from my job a while ago, and while I was trying to find another job, I spent more and more time with the animals in their environment, and just paid attention to them, watching all of the interactions and behaviors back and forth, with both the male side and the female side, and it inspired me to write about my observations while the animals and I bonded ... We developed a daily routine, and we got (and still get) along famously ... I was asked at the end of January 2014 to be a consultant for the company Rael works for, to help rebuild the transportation department, as I used to work there years ago ... Even though I was not technically an "employee" of the company, I have to endure all of the same attitudes and idiosyncrasies that the employees do ... In this time, I have seen what I was blind to, before, when staying employed and making regular money and dealing with the day to day was what I had to do ... Its still something I will do. ... out of greed ... I would like to get to a point in the near future, when Rael and I don't have to work, and can be full time alpaca shepherds, enjoying doing what is best for US, not some guy in a suit and tie ... When we deal with the sheer arrogant, condescending attitudes DAILY, the respite of the farm and the true blessing of all of our animals is our daily vacation ... Its the ones who have this over-inflated sense of entitlement and self worth that I feel sorry for ... They go home to their huge house with no yard; with no animals, and wait for their time to go to bed for the evening, only to wake and do the same thing the next day ... They count on the other humans in their lives to give them the self worth they so desperately need to keep going ... we don't need that ... The animals are the reason we keep doing what we do ... The keep us grounded with who we are to them, and who they are to us ... THEY matter most ... Not the suits who are so short sighted that the cant see to their next meeting ... The suits are in it for themselves only ... "What's in it for me..?" "What can you do for ME..?" ... These are people who do not and will NEVER share the joy of watching a cria being born, NEVER experience the wonder of watching these babies seeing and experience things for the very first time, NEVER do anything to help others without thinking about themselves first ... What an extremely monotonous, lonely, sad existence these people must lead ...

Experience ...

10:03 on a Monday night ... standing in the driveway for a breath of air, and you could swear you can hear your own heart beating. ... A lone truck on 86, a dog barks in the distance and ... .nothing. ... Still and quiet; another day put to bed ... A moment from my day ... Still trying to figure out why Eric ... A moment from another day ... I have realized one thing. That moments, are what makes us who we are as humans being on this planet ... These moments, good and bad, help us to learn and grow as individuals.. I can sit here all night and tell you all of my experiences here at the farm, but I choose not to ... Why..? You have yours, I have mine ... your experiences belong to you, because, you live them ... I live mine.. With every wonderful, fantastic, wobbly cria that start their journey here, with every sunset on the patio, watching the "kids" bump and crash into each other, with every shearing day and summer "get togethers" with like minded individuals ...

Sometimes the moments don't become wonderful memories. ... As with bringing life into our farm, there have been the moments that we have had to bury some within the herd ... Human and otherwise ... But, another lesson and unique experience that helps us become more sensitive, more caring, more mindful, and above all, more loving to the herd around you..

Living there for 12 years has taught me so much about life, my own and others, as well as a sense of inner peace, being with all of the animals ... I cherish the memories of the ones we have lost along the way; some expected, some not.. And I cherish the experience of what is still to be.. The unborn legends. ... All of it, is worth it.. That's been my experience ... And sometimes, just sometimes, the best experiences are when there's nothing going on at all ...

Divine Secrets of the Pa Ca Sisterhood …

When I spend time with the herd, I tend to gravitate toward the girls pen … The boys are separated like Chinese Fighting Fish, due to heightened testosterone levels, so we kinda have to do that to alleviate the bar brawl that would ensue should we get THEM all together.. Their own little cliques, herds within the herd …

But the girls …

They are all together in the same pen, and when their crias are born, the crias stay here as well, for the first 8-9 months of life if male, and permanently if female … The females who give birth to the males are initially accepted with the cria, until the male has become of "boy" age … Then both are "encouraged" to keep their distance … Once the male has been put in with the rest of the young males, then, and only then, will the mom be accepted back as a full member of the sisterhood again … Conversely, if a female is born, she is accepted right away and greeted triumphantly like a brand new princess by all of her new "aunts" … She is taught and shown the ways of the female side of the herd, always cognizant of her new place within the hierarchy. … The boys, when they become of age, are basically left to their own devices with the other males they now co-habitate with … No caring, no sharing, just having to deal with all of the things entailed with living with a bunch of testosterone laden young males; fights and sneak attacks, you know, that kind of thing. … The girls pretty much do everything together as a unit … Sometimes more loosely bound than others, but there is no mistaking that this group is aware of everything going on around them, at all times … They have a structure and a hierarchy that is unspoken but understood among them all … Every once in a while, there is a skirmish, or a test to the order of things, and these minor intrusions are quickly resolved and all is right with the herd … The males will fight until someone goes down, a more primitive and instinctual male thing to do … Males will meet a new addition and greet them with aggression and physical confrontation, whereas the girls will greet a new addition with inquisitiveness and wonder …

I believe the females are more structured simply because there are more of them in a localized space, and, at least on some level, understand the security and survival OF the herd is more important than their place in it … The adult females who are not pregnant tend to protect and play with the newborns, giving the exhausted mothers a chance to rest and catch their breath … One by one the new babies arrive and the herd grows … All are accepted … Even the boys.. initially … Until they get to be "boys" … Then its time again for the girls to be girls; ever vigilant in keeping the sisterhood safe and secure … The many become one, for the good of one, for the good of all …

The Feminine Divine …

After perusing some of the pages I have written so far, and most of the news articles I have browsed through, as well as a look back into my personal history, I have come to the conclusion that, well, for the most part, the troubles and acrimony within the world are because of the male ego. Males, and it doesn't matter what species, happen to enjoy the physical confrontation, and verbal abuse infinitely more than female counterparts. As I was growing up, I was privy to a lot of posturing, bravado, and basic, macho male bullshit from my father. But he was, and is, not the only representation of this particular Neanderthal dynamic. You don't have to go any further than the front page of any of the online news sites, or the first 5 minutes of any news program to see that.

I lived in a world where my mother was treated like a second class citizen, talked down to, made fun of, and basically treated like less of a human than her husband. Since then, I have seen this type of behavior play out with some of the males in my life. I guess, in some manner, its expected, as that's how they saw the females being treated in their lives.

In the realm of our 4 legged friends, I have noticed a completely different dynamic play out. With the dogs, there is a pecking order, to be sure, but any male dog, or strange male human, for that matter, that decides to wander onto this farm, will realize very quickly that they are unwelcome, and the "ladies" will represent that feeling at high velocity. The grandbabies are the same way, only within the confines of the 4 walls here: any male, strange or unknown, will feel the wrath of claws and teeth. No questions asked. With the llamas and the alpacas, males aren't even a consideration, unless its breeding time. That's what the males are good for. Period.. End of story ...

Don't believe me..? Ask them.

I have also noticed a dynamic here within these separate groups of females, that I have also seen in American society: By and large, females stick together, and operate for the good of the unit; the herd. They tend to work together toward a common goal, for the betterment of everyone. I'm not saying that all women and females act this way, but the greatest majority that I have seen, do. The great majority of males, the human animal and others, work for themselves, they want to be lauded as the hunter/gatherer/ breadwinner and the head honcho, if you will. They are the ones who wish to be waited on, feeling that sense of entitlement of "Well, I AM the man ... " There are exceptions to this as well, as the male friends I DO have now, will attest.

To the men that believe I have just invalidated my "Man Card", consider this:

Women are better at handling crisis situations,

Women are better at finances, by and large,

Women are better at talking to people and understanding their situation,

Women are better at treating people fairly, who have been through unfortunate circumstances in their lives, and are less willing to judge,

Women are smarter and can figure out solutions for the betterment of everyone involved,

Women will not screw over an entire group of people just for personal financial, or other, gain,

Women know what true love means, just ask any mother ...

Oh, and one last point, oh mighty superior males who read this:

If it wasn't for women, you wouldn't be here to spout the macho, Neanderthal bullshit that you do.

Be a partner, not a pain in the ass. Shut up and listen. You just might learn something.

Gratitude ...

Thank you. ... Gracias ... Grazie. ... All ways of showing appreciation ... So is this ...

I am grateful for all of the opportunities given to me in this life by my Creator, and all of the experiences that being an alpaca caretaker has offered to me, good and bad, that have shaped and molded me into the person I am today ... I am grateful, extremely grateful, for all of the people who hit "like" on one of my ramblings or one of our pictures, all of the people who have commented and actually understood what I was trying to say ... Sometimes I don't know what I'm trying to say ... I have learned and seen so much as a breeder, and I am thankful for a place like Facebook, so you can learn and see and meet others with like minds, others who say what you like, and like what you say. ... Its a joy to write and have someone else relate to it ... I am humbled by some of the comments I have received here and elsewhere ...

Grateful for all of the alpaca breeders and caretakers we have encountered in the last 10 years, unbelievably too numerous to mention, for all of the advice, the shearing days, all of the humor and good times, with a million more to come ... Every single one of them has taught us at least one good thing to implement into our farm, and with that knowledge, we are successful … Our success is because of your guidance, and we are grateful …

I am grateful for my family, and I am most appreciative and grateful, for my partner throughout this journey, Rael Reddick … Baby, you have been the rock throughout this whole journey, and it is by your 'firm, but loving' example that we are where we are today … I have learned so much with you throughout our lives together, and I look forward to the rest of my life with you.. … I love you …

And because I love you, I am going to start writing the book …

Balance …

To be able to get our home/farm life and professional, corporate existences in harmony, a lot has to go into that, both physically and mentally … there is the prep time involved in the morning, just trying to get motivated to go into an atmosphere, that, more often than not, CAN prove to be a bit toxic to the spirit … Rael and I choose to ignore the noise that is out there, and instead focus on the positive aspects of the day laid out for us … We see so many individuals within our day who are focused on the bottom line; on how to achieve the maximum effort from their people for the maximum profit margin, with as little effort given as possible from themselves … Quite sad really. … We focus on our jobs while we are within the confines of their building. … That's it … The minute we are out of there, we are focused on what the rest of this beautiful day has in store for us … we have the opportunity and privilege of being able to come to our home and congregate with the ones we really wanted to be with anyway … Our herd. … We are able to harmoniously blend the 2 worlds and have been able to make it work; for our spirits as well as the other spirits around us … We go to work so we can be able to enjoy the blessings that have been so richly bestowed on us … Would we prefer to spend all of our time here overseeing the herd..? You bet, but we are realistic enough in our thinking to know, that, the positions we hold within the business structure helps us to be able to keep this farm alive and vibrant. … And us as well. …

Now there are people within the alpaca collective who believe that the money means more than the animal, adopting, if you will, the "corporate business structure", employing others to take care of the herd. ... That's all fine, well and good, but we, personally, got into alpacas because the herd mentality and behaviors had us hooked the minute we did our first farm visit ... We believe in the spirit and harmony being the caretakers for our herd brings. ... While money and finances was a contributing factor in our decision, the community of the animals is what most attracted us, and has taught us the value of doing something, and being something better with our lives ... Learning and sharing, loving and caring for ALL of our animals has given us a better grasp on life in general. ... For me, communing with the herd has helped me understand my place in this existence, and given me a better understanding of community, true community that cannot and will never be duplicated in any office building. ... The animals provide the necessary balance and harmony in our lives to keep going; to keep striving to be something more than ourselves. ... As a herd. ... As a community ... A collection of spirits that give peace and unity to one another just by being there ...

Sacred Ground ...

As I was finishing chores this evening, the clouds lowered and fog started to envelope the countryside as the cool night air set in ... All of the visitors and residents were feeding peacefully, either in their shelter, or outside in the mist ... And as I walked around, you know, just checking, it struck me how absolutely peaceful and quiet it was across the entire property ... across the entire neighborhood ...

As I stood motionless in front of the girls pen, I listened and there was only the sound of a lone wind chime and the sound of a slight breeze through the fence ... No traffic, no dogs barking, no "drone" of any kind ... Just the silent acceptance of the herd at rest ... I started to think about our years here, and all of the babies born, and the lives lived right here on this little parcel of land ... Any animal, wild or domesticated, has found nothing but peace and tranquility here and for that, we are honored ... We have rabbits that run through and every September we have deer that bed down in our front yard ... The ones that are here to live and the ones that visit are respected and revered because they are part of the greater herd ... The ones that seek to do harm are quickly run off, so as not to endanger ANY member of the herd ...

I find pieces of what was, when I walk through the back pasture and I look around me and see what others before me must have seen: The most beautiful place on the planet ... Because the herd is here ... And the ones that have come before us are here ... We feel it in moments ... There is a distinct and powerfully positive energy here, like nothing we have experienced previously in our lives ... We are humbled ...

Value ...

Absolutely everything has value.. Either monetary, sentimental, spiritual, even perceived value ... We value friendships, we value the time spent together with each other.. We value physical, tangible things such as money, and all of the things that money can buy ... We value opinions from others and, in turn, hope that they can find some value in our opinions as well ... Everything, in one form or another has something of value; meaning something to each and every one of us ... And that value, like our fingerprints, is unique to each one of us as well ... Be it time spent with your Mom when you were younger, or getting married ... these have value that is spiritual, and cannot be bought at ANY price.. We believe the same with our farm ... The value of the experience ...

As alpaca breeders, we were in the business of buying and selling alpacas, breedings and all of the alpaca fiber and their associative products ... We attach a monetary value to each of these, but the intrinsic value of the animals as individuals goes far deeper than anything that money could buy ... There are a few animals that we have here that are not for sale at any price.. Why..? Because their value lies in something more to us than the almighty dollar ... It lies in the connection we have made with these individuals within the larger herd ... That doesn't mean that every individual

84

within the herd is any less loved or important.. Not by a long shot ... But, as alpaca breeders, we understand that we are in the "business" of selling animals and we try to get like minded individuals to see just what we see, and make the decisions for themselves ... We have people over and when its nice out, we let the girls out on the back pasture, and we all mingle with the animals ...

Peaceful and tranquil, listening to them graze and watching the babies run ...

The males are more laid back, and tend to pay a great amount of attention to the girls, on the rare occasion they are let out back ... Separately, of course ... They get the sides ...

That's their value, as the larger herd ...

We moved to the country several years ago to achieve this ... To be able to become something that is larger and more spiritual than we could ever hope to be ...

The larger herd ...

Individuals come and go within this journey we are all on, but the family, the herd stays intact ... The value in that is incalculable ...

We go through our lives doing the school, job, adult thing ... Getting by, muddling through, trying to make a difference ... The daily 9-5 has its moments, but, by and large, remains as monotonous as it sounds ... That's why we decided on alpacas all those years ago ... Neither one of us had a real "farm" existence prior to moving out here 9 years ago ... I grew up in the heart of old Aurora Colorado on a postage stamp lot, and the extent of the wildlife back then, was birds and squirrels ... Coming out here to Elizabeth, and making the decision to become the caretakers of these magnificent animals was something no one saw us doing; not in a million years.. We made the jump, knowing in our souls that this was the absolute best thing for us to do ... And every single day, watching the herd grow and interact with all of the others within these fencelines, has only proven and enhanced the original idea ... Every moment provides an education, not only for the mind, but for the soul and for our consciousness and attitude towards all living beings, right down to the 237 rabbits that frequent the back two and a half ... I am fortunate enough to be able to take pictures while I am within the herd, and share these images, these moments, these heartbeats with others, so that, maybe, just maybe, they will see what I see from within, and become more a part of their own herd from within as well ... These moments are just the everyday here on the farm ... These are just moments that happen ... Random small blessings within the everyday..

My blessing lies within the herd and my small piece within it ...

Reboot ...

Within experiences and everything we see, do and feel, there is change ... Sometimes subtle, sometimes drastic, and there are those that alter every-thing ... Thinking, doing, being, on every single level has been changed, trains of thought derailed and re-routed ...

A new reality ... A new headspace ... on every single level ...

We, as a family, as a farm, have decided to simplify our existence, to give attention to the things that matter, to consolidate and pare down ... The responsibility and great amount of physical labor this winter has taken it's toll, and as such, we have decided, as a farm and as a herd, that we are going to reduce the size of our alpaca herd by 70%, and concentrate more on rebuilding the herd from within, slowly, and share our animals with those that either have a farm now, or planning on being a caretaker for these magnificent animals ... As much as we love what we are doing within the herd construct, we feel it is time for us to simplify our everything ...

Reseed ... Restart ... Reinvent ...

Experiences on our journey have many lessons contained within ...

Some are subtle, some are drastic, and there are some that alter everything ...

In our lives we experience many things that help shape our thought processes and how we look at the journey.. People, places, things, adventures, all of these can color so many aspects of how we feel and act, as well as just being ... In an increasingly ugly and violent world we live in, it is inherent upon each of us to at least try and find some manner of beauty within it all..

As caretaker and guardian for our herd here, I have seen the good, the bad, the happy the sad, and sometimes we get to witness the primal beauty that blesses us within these fencelines ... Last week, I was witness to just such a blessing. I missed the birth of Picotani by mere minutes on Thursday, but I was able to see those first few minutes, the introductions of the herd to this new arrival, and, luckily, his first steps ... A happy, healthy baby boy ...

Friday, as I was cleaning pens, I noticed that Aurora, our 8 year old expectant girl, who, incidentally was also born on this farm, was overdue, and she started to hum more vociferously than I have ever heard her before ... Like she was in pain ... I watched as her entire being tightened up, and soon realized that she was having contractions. In the 10 years that we have had animals here, I had never seen any of them being born. I had always arrived after the fact, missing out on that opportunity to see what I had always wanted to see: new life from moment one. I kept a close eye on her, making sure there wasn't anything else going on that needed immediate medical attention ... She would rest and then pop up again, quite obviously uncomfortable, all the while quite "hummy" ... After about 20 minutes, I noticed that her vocalizations were getting closer together, and significantly louder ... After another half hour, the hums had been replaced by almost howls, she was so uncomfortable ... She finally stood up and lifted her tail, like she had to "go" ... That's when I saw the nose ... The rest of the head, and the front legs soon followed ... As the shoulders started to appear, I think it freaked her out a little, as she became extremely agitated, and started to walk briskly around the pen ... Worrying for the safety of the, as yet still not-yet-born cria, I managed to calm her somewhat, and assist with the completion of the delivery ... One final, very large push, and the baby was out.. I gently set this new life on the ground, and stepped back, not wanting to interfere any further in the progression of the natural order ... I was entirely mesmerized by the first movement of this new life on the ground, coughing and sputtering to clear his lungs, his airway, and his nose ... He shook his head to get all of the life giving amniotic fluid out of his ears and eyes, and get his bearings in this, all of a sudden bigger, brighter world.. I stood in absolute awe of the way his mother started to clean him, and watched as each member of the female herd came to him, one by one, to investigate the second new life in 2 days, enter into this ever evolving group ... Humming and cooing and introducing themselves to him, giving him that instinctive reassurance that he was now home, with them ... All of them paid absolutely no attention to me, as I took picture after picture of this new life, a witness to one of the most beautiful things I had EVER experienced outside of my own daughter's birth ... In those moments following, I was reduced to tears at the absolute beauty; an honor and pride inside my soul, that I had been able to witness this ...

In the days since I have watched as he took his first steps, and observed as these new eyes experienced absolutely everything for the very first time, and seeing this brand new being figure out his way around, all the while, side by side with his mother as she shows him how to be ...

Alive ...

CHAPTER FOUR

Earth

We the People ...

On a day like today, we will see the country and the people as a social landscape of ideas, fears, thoughts, threats and other things ... As we go forth into this day, we are either proud of our country and who the next leader is, or we feel threatened by the people and the chosen leader. That divides us exponentially. and, it is really quite sad. I have talked to people here in the community and they, just like this country, are divided in their thinking about the new resident of 2300 Pennsylvania Avenue, as well as the previous one. When we argue and fight and commit acts against our fellow human beings in the pursuit of being right, we lose all sense of who we are as individuals. That is the reason I choose not to enter into political conversations with people. I just listen. If I don't have an opinion on the matter, I don't vilify the other persons point of view. In America you say, think, feel, believe anything you want to believe, and that is one of the founding precepts of this country. With the advent of social media, and instant communication, people can share the views and beliefs to anyone who will listen. However, there are those who attack people for their opinions and belief systems, with an enormous sense of "I'm gonna prove you wrong, because you are full of shit ... "

We don't respect others anymore.

Those who don't believe the way we do, or don't look like us, or have a different orientation, sexual or otherwise, are viewed as a threat to our own existence and they must be eradicated from the planet. Why? Because, in this new age, apparently, different is wrong. That is why I don't enter into any conversations about these things. I let people go on their merry way, and yell and scream about how these differences are going to destroy us as a people; as a nation. I have seen too many things in my life, and talked to so many people in my life that believe this way, to believe that this is a way to achieve peace and harmony for the world, never mind the nation. Mob mentalities and hatred for the different is now the norm in the world.

..and that, my friends, is bullshit. Bullshit of EPIC proportions.

I may not always agree with someone, but I respect their existence enough to listen to what they have to say. I'm not going to attack them for their viewpoint, but try and understand exactly where they are coming from.

If you want a positive role model, be one …

Tranquility …

In this world of acrimony, greed and intentional pain, it can be difficult to try and achieve peace of mind, never mind peace of the heart and soul … I find that when I am writing or spending time with the animals, I can put a lot of that aside, and concentrate on what is needed for my own peace … Spending time with the dogs outside on a sunny day, or sitting with Isis and Thea on a cold day, or even in the evening when it's quiet, helps to calm the soul … When the world, real or virtual, keeps me up at night, I write … Sometimes I will sit at the laptop and just write about experiences in my day, thoughts about my past experiences, or what I need to do to become a better version of me …

Sometimes in silence, sometimes with the headphones on, listening to native flute music or the myriad of nature recordings I have. This is where the book is coming from; these late night scribblings about, well, everything. That's where I find my solace; within … Life has taught me to listen to the inner rumblings and ramblings of 50+ years on the planet, and the lessons, even the smallest ones, brought to the forefront of my consciousness with something as simple as being with the animals, large and small, and the quiet …

Silence the storm and quiet the mind … peace will follow …

Island time …

When we decided that we were going to forgo the traditional Christmas in 2016, we contacted Scott and Susan Mikulecky about the availability of their beach house in St Croix; Blue Turtle Beach House ... Luckily, fortunately and quite blessedly, we were able to procure the rental of the house for the 2 weeks before and between Christmas and New Years. We, as a family, just didn't want to deal with the holidays here, without Eric ... It was already going to be difficult, as the first Christmas without him, so we decided to be somewhere warm, without all of the trappings of the holiday as reminders ...

So we left a couple of days before Christmas, out of the grey of Colorado and set forth to the warm of St. Croix ...

Once there, we were floored by the absolute beauty and lush greenery that surrounded us. This was the perfect place for us to settle in and be together, as a family, to quietly reconnect with ourselves individually, and as a unit ... There were times that we swam in the ocean, there were times that we travelled the island to check out all of the sights, colors and textures, and there were times when we each drifted off to ourselves to mourn the loss, and reflect on our lives up to this point in time ...

The beauty of the people on the island was just as magnificent. As we travelled around Frederiksted, we encountered people who were grateful, not because of what they owned, but because of who they were and they were blessed just to be ... Amazing, in this world today ...

For me personally, I took a lot of pictures, both with my camera and my soul, enveloping my entire being in the moments of tranquility that this oasis has to offer. While Rael and Emelie were collecting sea glass and shells, I was collecting sunsets and images of the diamonds on the water; images that now take me back to this time, that keep me warm as the Colorado winter remains cold and unsettled ...

At the time, it was difficult for me to put into words exactly what I was feeling during these moments. Upon reflection and perusing these images once again, the clarity of where we were and what we experienced is real. We went there to become one as a family again; to regroup, to re-establish the family bond, and I think that we did that. We laughed together, we cried together, but we were TOGETHER ... And while we went together,

I believe that it was important for us, as individuals, to reconnect with what we needed, and still need to feed our personal selves ...

I, personally, came out of this with a greater respect and awe of the natural world, of the beauty of things created by the Creator. Colors, textures, sounds, silences that I had never experienced in my existence before ... ever. I also came away with a greater sense of being, of listening, of understanding the soul ...

Every moment, every experience, everyone who has ever been in your life, help to mold you into who you become ...

How you choose the lessons, is entirely up to you ...

Be the best ...

Be the blessed ...

There is only beauty in the natural world around us ... The only ugly within the world is created by the arrogance of the corporate machine and of the ones within our existence who seek to better their bank accounts at the expense of the natural world ... The Creator made all of the wonders of nature, and everything in it, and while we are also made by the Creator, there are those who seek to make money off of these creations by becoming ego-driven enough to think that they can improve upon the natural beauty around us by creating their own ...

Nature does not charge a fee ...

Nature does not have iron bars or artificial means to control the living species within the planet ...

Nature does not discriminate ...

Nature does not need control ...

Nature lives ...

Nature breathes …

Nature has a soul, and if we, as humans can realize that, we can make that connection which is so vital to the propagation of all species for their, and our survival …

Enjoy the beauty of the natural world within the natural world …

Respect the connection …

Opening the mind, tears down a life of expectation, and perception … Once the decision is made to accept more, respect more and expect less, the idea of ideals vanishes, and the mind becomes as vast as the blue …

Warm and sunny, isn't only the weather … It can be your outlook on even those days that seem dark and gloomy …

Anyone can be a cloud …
Be the sun …

When you feel peace and tranquility within, time stops …
My soul is grateful for these moments …

To see the beauty in everything, all you have to do is open your eyes …
And your heart and soul …

To be one with it all, you must experience it all …

I don't have to like it, but I accept it …

I respect it …

Accept existence …

Or ...

Expect resistance ...

Open your mind, or close your options ...

Peace ...

The ocean, I have found, pulses and undulates like a beating heart ... The life surrounding it feeds on that planetary heartbeat and thrives ... From the smallest fish to the largest whale, life thrives and adapts, quite successfully, to that heartbeat ... Calm or storm, life adapts ...

Life thrives ...

When you show appreciation to another, it helps them feel good ... It also speaks to who you are as an individual soul ...

Be thankful for everything ...

And everyone ...

I am thankful for you today ...

Peace ...

Find something ...

Find something that moves you ...

Find something where passion is the only word ...

Find something that connects with you ...

Find something that you are, not something that you do …

Find something larger and infinitely more important than your ego …

Find something that evolves and, in turn helps us evolve for the better …

Find something that makes your heart sing; that helps to cleanse the soul …

Find something that can change the world, one human at a time …

Find something positive and uplifting … .

Find something about yourself, when you decide to

Find something …

Always be grateful for the blessings of now …

A year in the life …

365 days ago right now, we were in Peru, starting to immerse ourselves within the culture, the spiritual, the tradition and the absolutely all encompassing experience of it all.. Starting to open our minds to the things we were seeing, synapses firing, ideas percolating … Colors, textures smells, people, places. … So many, so many, so different from what I have known in this life. … Observances in this time that have helped mold my interior, especially the spiritual interior … You could feel the difference in consciousness there … In the cities or in the Highlands, there were acts of humanity, acts of community, acts of trust of someone from a different culture, connections on so many levels …

The blessing of that experience, that ENTIRE experience, has taught me, has shown me, a way to act, react and deal with, well, life … and everything in it … Trust in the traditions and the ancestors …

Believe ...

Honor ...

Gratitude ...

A whole new frame of reference for when we would return here later in the month ...

With all that has transpired in that 365 days, this time in Peru was essential, was absolutely vital to helping us through this part of the journey ... Within this year, I have learned, I have been enlightened, I have been tested, and I will continue to evolve ...

Continue to evolve ...

With every lesson

there is a reason,

with every reason,

there is a lesson ...

Be more about WHO you have in your life, instead of WHAT you have in your life ...

2 weeks ...

That's how long I have been able to stay here within the homestead, venturing out into civilization just long enough for the odd job interview and Home Depot.. And while I know finding gainful employment is imperative at this time, it has been nice to be able to have the house to myse ... ., I mean share the house with Thea and Isis. ... It has given me time to get some things done around here in preparation for the coming winter, and it has given me ample time to roam around within my own head, heart, and take a peek into my soul … Listening to the sounds of the outside, and being committed to the sun, as the warmth and bright have been very healing to me.. It's almost as though I have been reintroduced to myself …

The experiences we have within our lifetime, shape and mold the person we eventually settle on becoming … Settle on becoming … We let all of the bad experiences infiltrate our entire being, and we close up like a flower at dusk.. We SAY that we're going to reach out, but … We let these events, happenings, incidents, define our very being, and I can completely understand how the darkness can overwhelm, desensitize, and even consume a person whole … It is very easy to just let it happen, let the anger and sadness and darkness win.. I was there, and even now there are still times where the dark starts to creep in, but I try to diffuse it, spending time with his girls, our girls and the light of the animals here … Re acquainting myself with the outside; the sights, sound, scents … The colors and textures of everything living … even as the leaves start their descent from their treetops, there is a certain, inherent beauty in this as well … Daily, subtle reminders that the evolution is still in progress …

I choose to go on and try to continue Eric's commitment to the nature of life and the life of nature …

Peace …

Begin by saying thank you for everything you have …

Changes …

In the attempt to "redecorate" my headspace into something more positive and forward-moving, I have had to rethink a lot of my past and my reactions to these things, as they influence how I react to things now as a so-called "adult" … I have had to start to re-think Energy from an entirely different and enlightened perspective; how positive energy begets positive energy, as well as negative energy.. I have started measuring my reactions to different situations, and thinking them through before I react. I have learned that the response is infinitely more memorable than a reaction … (Thank you for that one, Rael …

A potentially negative situation can be redirected to the positive by merely looking at the situation differently. Identifying the problem is easy; its the solution that needs to be addressed …

Retraining my mind and rethinking everything, it feels like i am at the beginning of school again; the mind, a blank slate, waiting to fill it with absolutely everything we wanted and needed to keep going in our lives … Fresh eyes upon knowledge … Learning, absorbing, feeling …

Taking time to remember the past and all of the lessons the past has to teach me …

Positive begets positive …

ReEvolutionary Process …

In the beginnings of cellular life, we are fed and nurtured within the womb of the mother; shielded from the outside and the cold, within a warm place, a safe place … Then, when Nature deems it necessary, we are born into the great big expanse that is to become our life … We learn and grow by the individual experiences we have, and, eventually, at least TRY, to become the person we want to be. As we become adults, we are exposed to completely, and not so completely, different experiences and lessons than we navigated through in our youth … There is more seriousness; more consequence, and we adjust our behavior accordingly … Most of the time … Ok, some of the time …

Some of the experiences that we go through can change the path; deviate from the norm, if you will … We have THOSE adult experiences that have a profound effect on who we are, but we are able to "right the ship" and press on, moving forward. The path is a little deviated, but still going in the general vicinity as before, with a few edits..

Then there is an event, an experience ...

In the aftermath, I, and we, felt the need to cocoon ourselves, within ourselves and this sanctuary ... Much like the womb, the family and the farm, provides warmth, safety and is nurturing for the soul ... Then, when Nature deems it necessary, we are re-born into the great big expanse that is to become the rest of our lives ...

The fog is lifting, and the mind is starting to re assimilate to life, and the path comes a little more into focus with each passing day.

I am learning ...

I am dealing ...

I am growing ...

The evolution continues ...

In beauty there is wisdom ...

In wisdom there is beauty ...

4 basic truths about me ...

1. No one will ever be able to offend me, hurt my feelings, or insult me anymore ...

2. The ones I love, cherish, and honor will be protected, to the bitter end ... No matter what ...

3. I have come to this point in my life, and I have seen so many things, enjoyed the company of so many people, so many memories, so many

blessings … I am grateful … but I recognize I am incomplete … and I will continue to evolve …

4. Don't bullshit me.. I hate that … straight up, no chaser … I'm a big boy now … I'll be honest, you be honest … that's it..

The ones who matter, remain..

Enlightenment …

I have heard, don't know if it's true or not, but … true enlightenment is achieved right before you meet your maker …

I believe that events and experiences that we encounter on our journey, can and do assist in not only helping us become the truest and purest form of ourselves, but also the mindframe and inner peace that we accept into our heart and soul …

We are raised in a certain way: the way our parent[s] decide on the who, what, where, when, and how, and that is the basis for the "interior decorating" of our headspace; our first apartment, if you will … I was told by my father how I was to going to act, what I will believe, and the people I was going to associate with … It's important to note, that, unfortunately, my father was from the old school; the women were possessions to be owned, and the kids were nothing more than poorly paid employees who did the fathers bidding. Only after our obligations were completed were we were allowed to go outside with our friends and just be kids.. It was what he knew as a kid, and, he thought that "If it was good enough for me, it's good enough for these kids … " As I grew and expanded my friendship base in school, away from the domineering hand of the old man, I learned things that were directly contradictory to what I believed was the way everything was supposed to be … New ideas, ideals, and differing points of view … These are the things that, privately, my mother encouraged: free thinking, individuality, and most important, tolerance and love for everyone, regardless … Mom is the most influential person in who I have become, and the catalyst for the husband and father I have become as well … She taught us, not only religion and the importance of belief, but spirituality as well … And later in our lives, she showed me the importance of honesty, true honesty and the integrity to stand up for myself and what I believe in …

When Dad died, it freed all of us from his macho bullshit belief system.

When Mom died, it freed her from the pain of cancer, but it did something else quite unexpected: I feel her soul has become a part of me as well, helping to empower me in my quest for internal peace.

When Eric died, everything I knew was blown apart and scattered everywhere. In the time since, I have become a different individual; beliefs have been challenged, ideas have hatched, relationships and alliances have come into greater focus and clarity, and I have relied on my spirituality to attempt to find what eludes most of us: tranquility and harmony in my soul.. I question everything now, and I have no room in my headspace for bullshit, and all of the accoutrements that inevitably go along with it … I have withdrawn from the "social scene" as it were, being especially mindful of everyone around me, and us, whenever we go out into society. It is only when we are together, in the fresh air on our farm or in the mountains that my mind can quiet and I am able to listen to the voices in the wind, and the heartbeat of the earth around me … It is here, away from the constant drone of the "civilized" world, that I can find even the briefest of respites from the cluttered mess behind these eyes …

The path to enlightenment is not an easy stroll paved in gold.

It is an uneven, rocky, sometimes dangerous and maddening trek, littered with obstacles and mis-steps throughout. I am still trying to stay on this path and reconcile absolutely everything I am, everything I believe, and I keep striving; climbing to that place where I am hoping that the light will continue to show me the way … I will walk this path for as long as necessary, no matter how hard, no matter how dangerous, finding pieces of myself until I am complete.

I will keep going …

Shit I have learned since December 28th, 2015 ...

Aside from my Facebook family, I have managed to be ostracized by, all of my blood family completely. It hurt for a moment, but I quickly realized something: blood relatives do not always mean family. The blood that understood me the best and the ones that showed genuine concern for our well being have passed, and the ones that are left are only interested in one thing ... themselves.

2 brothers, that, at one time, I thought, had our welfare in their best interest, have been nowhere to be found, and cannot even give us the time of day now ...

Whatever ... I know who cares and who REALLY matters ...

Members of the Circle, some of whom I have never met even once, have reached out and given me and us their unconditional support and love. That means more to me, and to us, than anyone could possibly imagine. You are more Family to me than the ones I grew up with ...

I have learned that the animals, especially the dogs, are infinitely more in tune with how we feel on an everyday basis ... More than the humans we physically interact with on a daily basis ... The animals seem to just KNOW, being "right there" when it is needed at that moment the absolute most.

I have learned, and watched, as his girls, Isis and Thea, have grieved tremendously, and still do. But their acceptance of us, as their new family, becomes stronger with each passing day. Their comfort level with their new surroundings also increases with every sunrise; every sunset. While the trust is still being constructed, it IS being constructed still, there is an understanding: an understanding that they have a permanent home here, and that we will protect them ... at any cost.

I have observed the human animal throughout this time, and I can tell, at least I think, who "gets" me and understands who I am and who I'm trying to be. I have also observed, and this is the majority of the face to faces I have had, that people are immensely interested in themselves, and in what they have been doing for the last forever … You see it in the media all of the time, and there's a part of you that thinks: " Well, it's the media, and they always blow things out of proportion …"

No … Sadly, the media are "dead nuts on" with this characterization …

I have seen a table with 10 people seated around it, all obviously there together, every single one, with their faces buried in their phone, "talking" to the ones within, and not paying attention to the others sitting right next to them …

I have seen a lady lose her fucking mind because the wait in line was more than 5 minutes …

I have seen people lash out at the cashier at Wendy's because they didn't get their Frosty expeditiously enough …

On the flip side of that coin, I have witnessed school age children, in their heightened state of "school's out", immediately stop their horse play, to help an elderly man cross a busy street, showing respect and honor in doing so …

I have seen a man give an animal a second chance at a life, at love, at trust, for both of them, and the connection forged since they met.

We have had individuals come up to us and offer their condolences and support who never even met Eric, but knew of him through friends or whatever … These small blessings and acts of grace give me a bit of hope that, maybe, just maybe, as a species, we CAN care … and that matters.

I have learned to tune out the crap, and try to grasp the good in every, EVERY circumstance.. I have always said that there is a lesson in every experience that we encounter in our lives..

It is what we choose to do with these lessons that can "make or break" us as individuals …

How we evolve is ultimately up to each and every one of us..

Choose wisely …

When "man-made" has more intrinsic and monetary worth than "nature created", that's when we have lost our way …

MindScapes …

When I feel the pressure and stress of the typical day, I find I can escape with the help of some headphones and a large selection of things to listen to. From the comedy of Monty Python, to the dark twisted metal of Slipknot, and everything in between, I can go anywhere within my psyche and create that temporary space that cocoons me away from the world and all of the blah blah within it … These auditory respites from the everyday help to alleviate the pressure, the heightened emotional input, and just your everyday, run of the mill bullshit … Music helps to color my headspace for the appropriate moments, creating the mood for the response … Different, varied tempos, time signatures, instrumentation, style, presentation, all of it, has helped me in some form, start to rebuild the infrastructure of the mindset again …

Writing is starting to help as well …

There have been so many times that I have wanted to put thought to "pad", but so many instances of darkness would invade the thought, that writing it down seemed so counterproductive to the healing process, as well as the general message of positivity and tolerance …

Amidst the spiritual and emotional chaos of the last 6 months, there have been glimpses of light, of purpose, of carrying on and moving forward …

That's what needs to be written here: words that heal, words that elicit a memory, words of experience and lessons …

Embrace the now, and those within it ...

HeadSpace ...

Getting there ... Many interior travels have begun, with more as yet to be embarked upon ... Looking back, attempting to live in the now, and starting to formulate the future ... Using the lessons we have learned from before, adapting them to the now ...

Adaptation,

Modification,

Simplification,

Rediscovering the importance of together,

Purpose and meaning,

But every last bit of my 50 years on this journey, has been, and will continue to be, another lesson ...

Learning, and acquiring knowledge, thought, and conjecture, forming the basis and the infrastructure of the headspace..

Every thought, word, deed, experience, interaction, all creating who we are, right at this moment ...

Although the support system we have been blessed with has been and continues to be wonderful, invariably, inevitably, ultimately, the care and upkeep of my headspace, is mine ...

A work in process ... but forward..

Ever forward ...

Changed …

People we know have approached Rael and Emelie recently, and asked them if I was ok. A perplexing question, on the surface, but necessary, from their standpoint … When asked why they didn't just come to me and ask, my wife and my daughter were told that I was "unapproachable", or they "didn't want to make me angry" by simply asking how I was doing … Understandable, given the circumstances … Rael and Emelie have been more than magnanimous in being able to talk to people and really being able to share their emotions and feelings with people, either face to face or on the phone. I, on the other hand, have been able to completely express myself only in person, and only to a select group of individuals in Colorado, and a few out-of-state Facebook friends while at the Great Western Alpaca Show.. Other than that I have tried to convey messages in my Facebook timeline, to mixed effectiveness, it turns out. I am extremely grateful for the people who have reached out to Rael and Emelie during our journey the last 6 months; the ones who talked, who cared enough to listen and have genuinely concerned themselves with our welfare.

With recent world events and my entire mindset, it has become increasingly necessary to "wall myself off" from the people who I used to call friends, and in a couple of instances, family, to feel safe within my own head. Eric's passing has made me re-evaluate my entire existence, and, consequently, everyone in it. Outside of Facebook, I have very few friends these days, and it is all because of my issues, not theirs. In the past year I have managed to ostracize almost everyone on my own personal "friends list" here. I just feel, that, at this point in my life, I have to keep the ones I trust closer to me, and eliminate those that really couldn't be bothered. These are people who I used to consider "family" … In some ways it's really kind of sad, but in others, completely necessary to me and my own sense of internal security.

I do not, can not and will not speak for Rael and/or Emelie here, as they are handling all of this in their own way, and it is not my right to do so. I can only speak to my own situation and my own circumstances.

The people I trust and can truly call my friends, know exactly who they are, and where they stand with me. If any of my Facebook friends ever have a question about any of this, all you will have to do is ask ...

You are part of the Circle, and, as such, I consider you my family of friends.

Looking inside ... finding things within yourself that you had either forgotten about, or had no idea that they were there ... Remembering times of import ... milestones ... the abstract, unusual, random times ... The thoughts that pour into my psyche from time to time, help me to focus; focus on what is truly important, and just what is trivial ... I am trying to take stock of myself; of my life to this point, and noticing the changes that are coming over me now ... I feel older ... I feel, in certain circumstances, that I have to be honest with people ... REALLY honest ... Not to be mean, but to make absolutely sure that they understand exactly where I, where WE, are coming from, and where we are at ... I feel as a guardian for my family, maybe more now than at any other time ... That's what's important to me ... Helps keep me upright ...

For now ...

If they're important, let them know ... always let them know ... .

Mile Markers ...

Its continually amazing to me that the human body and spirit can go from the highest most beautiful points in the journey, and shortly thereafter, the absolute depths and darkness that only nightmares are made of ... And in both instances, getting to touch the face of God ... I turned 50 in October 2015 and that gave me an opportunity to reflect and assess my existence up to that point in time; the journey so far, if you will ... There are landmark events on everyone's path: 1st birthday, First Communion, turning 16 and getting your license, Graduation, 21 and now you are an adult, that kind of thing ... Events that, when I turned 50, I was able to look back from a completely different vantage point than I thought possible.. Jaded by time,

and experiences since, but true to the original memory, if only slightly …
It was cathartic and quite humbling to look back at the person I used to
be, and take stock and be extremely grateful for the experiences and person
I have become … mostly.. 50 years, I thought … .wow … never thought
I would be here … A wonderful herd.. A wonderful, happy, healthy family … I stood in the driveway late that night and thanked my Mom …
asked her to put in a good word for me to the Big Guy, you know … I
saw 10 million stars, as the night was black as coal … And I thanked my
Creator for bestowing the most wonderful blessings upon me; infinitely
more than I could ever deserve … Ever …

November came and we embarked on our 2 week adventure to Peru …
We saw things and had experiences within the physical realm, but the
spiritual realm within the people and the culture, opened my eyes and
my heart to the simplicity of life, and holiness of purpose that the people
of the Highlands and the towns alike, shared with us on our journey …
When you experience something like that, from a physical standpoint, it
is extremely exhausting … But, and I say this from MY headspace here,
I came back spiritually enlightened, and awakened again … My entire
approach to everything was altered for the better … We came home and
enjoyed the holidays with family, extended family, and some very close,
dear friends … We shared our pictures and our stories at Thanksgiving,
and spent a nice, quiet family Christmas at home … Life is good …

I sit here many months removed from that Christmas … I look at everything that has happened since, and I cry … I am convinced that the
awakening experienced in Peru has a lot to do with the fact that I am still
upright … My entire existence took a shovel to the face on December 28th
2015 … In these 50+ years, I have never, EVER had ANYTHING affect
me like this … Emotionally, physically, spiritually, physiologically altered
for the rest of forever … The type of pain that never really goes away …
The type of sadness and despair that lurks around, everywhere, just out of
sight … We battle through everyday, from first light to goodnight … And
we will wake up tomorrow and do it again … and again …

I stand in the driveway now and look out into the jet black sky and there are 10 million stars, like diamonds in the expanse … And I listen for Eric, hoping, praying that he's still here, I just haven't felt him yet …

50 years I thought … Wow. … Never thought I would be here … .

Primal …

Pack

Pride

Herd

Tribe …

A sense of personal community … A place where we actually belong.. A place where we can feel safe and know, absolutely know, that we are accepted and loved … That feeling is reciprocated in every instance … During the late Spring and Summer, when all can be outside and create the hum of the new season.. Last years crias are this years yearlings, full of energy and ready to run and jump and explore outside the confines of their semi-ample pen … They, as we, are ready for the cold and gray of Winter, to turn to the warmth and sunshine, the annual promise of Spring … As the days get longer and warmer, we are able to get outside for longer periods and spend more time with the herd, reacquainting our souls after the cold of Winter.. We have been blessed to be able, on those cold snowy days, to be able to socialize and connect more fully, with the pack within the herd: canine division … During the dark and cold of the last 8 weeks, we have been blessed with the care and concern, as well as the extraordinary sense of security, that our girls have bestowed upon this family, this herd … Sable, Taima, Maddie, and even the puppy, Phoebe, have been ever present in every move we make, be it inside, or when I go out to do chores … They are keeping an eye on all 3 of us, ensuring that all is OK, and we are safe and sound … They have even made sure that the 2 newest members of our herd, Isis and Thea, are secure and safe.. When we are away at work, they roam the back two and a half, keeping order and making absolutely

110

sure that the property is locked down ... When they are with us as we rest, they sense what is happening here ... I think that they could possibly be more in tune with the feelings and emotions that occasionally wash over us within the space of any given moment, than even we are ...

These dogs, these girls, these saviors of our souls, have my undying respect, love and loyalty for the beings that they are, for the moments that they have comforted us as only they could do, for all they mean to my family, their pack, our herd ...

The first grasses of the year are starting to brave the cold air and peek out, impatiently waiting for the first warmth of Spring ... But until then, we will be here, in the comforting warmth of community, with the ones that know; the ones that continue, the ones that keep us grounded, centered, sane ...

Right now, that's enough. ... We're good here ...

Colors ...

Physical death does strange things to people ...

Turns the insides of the closest to the deceased, inside out ... Close relatives act as relatives act ... Family that was here for the Holidays, cut short their vacation to come here and stay with us to help and comfort ... Thank you Gary and Barb Watts ... You both were angels of Mercy to us in an impossibly dark time ...

Close friends of the family can go one of two ways I have found:

They get closer and go way above and beyond to help and do absolutely anything in the spirit of family ...

or

They contact us, usually email or text, once or twice, keeping a distance either out of respect, or out of fear. … Fear of the sadness … And that is completely ok … Why..?

Because, as it turns out, with physical death, comes ultimate truth. How we react when someone dies, whether they are a son, a mother, a grandmother, it doesn't matter who.. … … How we react is instant, and those closest to you will rally around and surround you with love … The closest. … The ones who drop everything and just be there … That is instant, that is who they are and what we mean to them … The ideal truth … A truth of love and compassion and actual caring for someone else in need of comfort, other than themselves … We have found these blessings in abundance in our hour of need … These are people that have become members of our family, even though not related …

The flip side of that coin, are the ones who, until this, have said that we were like family to them, that if we ever needed anything that they would be right there …

Um …

If that's how they deal with this, well, that tells me everything I will ever need to know about what their truth is …

The content of your character is defined by how you treat others …

The ones related to you really hurt, though …

But, there again, THEIR truth …

We know who matters …

The circle has been adjusted accordingly …

Absolutely one moment at a time … .one step at a time … from sunrise to moonrise, watching, observing, as life goes on outside these eyes … Meanwhile behind these eyes is a tornado ravaged trailer park, familiarity and some semblance of an order, strewn about like so many childrens toys after a temper tantrum ... I walk around the trailer park within my head and I pick up remembrances at the most unusual times and "places" ... These I hold on to like they are made of gold ... Slowly, painfully,there is a sense that order will come..

"The New Normal"

Not really a term I am fond of, because, what is "normal" ...?? "Normal" is living by the script, I feel ... There really is no normal, if you think about it ... All there really is, is reality ... My reality, and how i choose to accept, deny, deal with, abandon, or embrace my reality, is really up to me ... As in our life here, I must adapt to any and all situations on the farm, in the home, within the family ... within the herd, for the success and survival of all ... You find a way. ... Period ... Improvise, overcome, adapt ...

Is it difficult..? Yep ...

Is it short term ...? Nope ... Not by a long shot ...

Some of the points along the journey are fraught with danger, treacherous caverns, and things unspeakable ... But that is why they are POINTS on a JOURNEY ... We were never given the keys to the easy life, so we must carry our own packs, and venture forth, taking time every now and again, to remember to breathe ... The easy life may get you there faster, but there's a lot to be said for carrying your own pack and creating your own journey ... Not scripted ... Improvised at this point ...

But still on the journey ...

21 ...

Emelie,

21 years ago today, the Creator blessed us with you, our baby girl ... With everything, absolutely everything that you have had to endure throughout your life, you never complained when you had every reason to.. You have made our lives an infinitely better and richer place to be, just by your mere presence ... You have taught this old man how to honor and respect all things living, and your interactions with our animal friends, of all species, fill us with wonder and amazement ... You are a gift to us; the ultimate blessing that has helped us become the people we are today ... your mother and I have learned so much from you and your brother; things we never would have learned otherwise ...

Our love and admiration for you, knows no bounds ... You are a bright and shining example of the younger generation, caring and sharing who you are, and always helping those less fortunate ...

We are very proud of the young woman you have become, and we will love you until the end of forever ...

Happy Birthday baby ... Our Little Valentine ...

Archive ...

When I first got on to Facebook, it was at the behest of both my children, and gentle nudging from Rael ... I wouldn't know what to say, or how to say it, or make any sense at all ... And she told me to just write what I feel, so, I did ...

In the process of cleaning the basement a few years ago, she stumbled upon an old notebook of her writings from her adolescence ... We stopped cleaning for a few moments, and perused some of this hidden treasure ... She writes so beautifully and conveys emotion so well, but her method is handwritten and more personalized to the individual ... Through reading what she has written, and constantly asking her advice, I hope I have been able to keep up ... I attempt to convey an emotion, a temperature, a sense, painting a picture for your minds eye to see ... and, on some level, feel ...

Rael has been able to do just that, on an epic level, as she has hand written almost 100 thank you cards, letters and notes to all of the wonderful people, family, and close friends who have sent condolences ... Her eloquence and raw inner truth in what she writes to all who grieve with us ... Her strength through all of this, and being able to do that ...

Writing through emotion is extraordinarily difficult when it is this intense. ... Conveying emotion in what is written can be impossible ... for me.. Verbalizing lately has been next to impossible ... Writing has proven to be at least somewhat therapeutic, as I have time and a space to type, I can take my time and hash out a thought, add, delete, whatever ... as it comes to me, in a lot of cases. ... We also have the added benefit of 5 acres and alpacas; llamas, and dogs. ...

Oh, and cats ... a different headspace than the regular, larger city, covenant controlled, 9 to 5er's. ... We were there ... We ARE here ... Spiritual people in their place of spirit ... Space is here, and we can go to the silence when necessary. ... Our church is thanking the Creator when the sun starts its warming ascent on to the landscape, fresh cup of coffee in hand, enveloping ourselves in the sounds of the world waking up ...

I just want to convey a message, a feeling, an experience ... and make people think ...

Have you ever been experienced? Well ... I have ...

10:35 ...

Can't sleep ... mind going a million miles an hour ... its quiet. ... A lone dog barks in the distance ... about 5 degrees out. ... It's still ... and snowing ...

You can almost hear the planet breathe when it's this quiet ...

I find myself most content when it's dark ... That is when my mind is the clearest, and I am able to form an Extended Release Cognitive Thought ... When everything must sleep for the night, and rest ... Simply rest ... Everyone is asleep and breathing deeply ... I see all of them and I am grateful for the opportunity, the duty and the honor of being here, among these beings ... As a husband, as a father, as a caretaker of souls, I watch over them, when they rest from watching over me.. Amidst the actual darkness and the personal one, this is when I can breathe; when I know all are here, all are safe, and all are somewhat content ... A moment of peace, of silent tranquility, of rest ...

The evolution of self ...

The only time in our lives that our soul is 100 percent pure, unadulterated by the experience of traveling on this leg of the journey, is about the first 20 minutes that we begin this journey on Earth ... We are brought home from the hospital and loved and fed and entertained and disciplined and told what we need to know to be able to survive out there in the big bad world ... My father was a big proponent of physical dominance over the family, and we were brought up as such ... I was lead to believe, quite foolishly, that a physical confrontation was the ultimate resolution to a conflict ... My mother disagreed vehemently, albeit in quiet, due to my father's penchance for anger ... The older he got, the bigger we got, and although we were now bigger than him, we had it ingrained in our psyche that he was always stronger; he was the MAN of the house, and if you don't like it, you can get the fuck out ... I wish I were making this up ... But even in the church, we were taught that the man is the driving force in the relationship, and he is the king of the household, and all of that pseu-do-macho archaic bullshit ... My mother, more so than us, was treated like a second class citizen in our house, and i just remember that from a very young age, I always thought there was something dreadfully wrong with that ... Cook, clean, entertain, babysit, sit and pay all of the bills herself, everything ... .everything ... And, as kids, you're really not supposed to notice that kind of stuff ... I did. ... My mother endured a LOT of crap from my old man, and she has my utmost respect, and my undying love, for staying with him, so that her children could learn from his mistakes, and, hopefully, maybe, one day, they would have that opportunity to be a good husband and a good father to their kids and atone for his transgressions ... That's all ...

There is no dominance within these fencelines, and, aside from the minimal skirmishes between the boys out back, there is an air of harmony here ... I have learned forgiveness for the past, and also thankfulness for it as well ... Why..? Those times are the lessons that are the most important: the ones on how NOT TO BE ...

I actually, regretfully, tried my fathers "raising" technique on Eric when he was young ... You know, the "fear of God" technique ... That's what we called it. ... Didn't work ... from day One. ... He just wanted to be heard, so I tried something radically different for the men in my house, and actually LISTENED to what he had to say ... He actually helped me become a better father by his insight and his spiritual connection with all things outside ... I listened to him, which, in turn, helped me listen to Emelie better ... They have taught me a tolerance and understanding, that has enlightened me tremendously in my personal journey ...

None of the better half, so far, of this journey would have ever been possible without my better half, Rael ... At the time in my life that I was at a HUGE crossroads, and she came into my life, like an angel. ... She saved me from myself and pulled me in a new and better direction than the one I was headed on ... No longer fueled by drugs and alcohol, she opened my eyes to so many different possibilities, and led to opening so many doors for me; for us ... Family camping trips, fishing in Alaska, the Chaku in Picotani, none of that would have been possible ...

I am forever grateful and humbled to her for allowing me the absolute honor of being a father to her children ... I know, I know, I had a part in all of this, but ... I do understand the connection of a mother and her children ... I get that. ... I am just so blessed to able to have seen what I have seen and experienced all I have in my life ...

The story behind my eyes, and the evolution of my soul is ongoing in so many ways … The things I have seen, and what I have witnessed in my 50+ years has, I believe, not only changed and molded my psychological and spiritual belief systems, but I believe that there are events in our lives that affect and alter us, right down to the DNA … Events so large that they are monuments within our life … Marriage, birth, death, transitions of major consequence … All have impact on who we are and who we are to become …

The evolution will not be televised, but it will be broadcast …

Sacred Wavelength …

When we meet people that we get along with and actually enjoy spending time with, we say that we are on the same wavelength … Agreeable, complementary, just a joy to be around … All of us have these in our lives, our best friends and the people who are "with you". … As there are a couple of people in my life that I feel this way around, I must say that the ones I feel MOST "like minded" with, are the animals … They have the right idea, living and grazing with the ones who matter within the herd; like minded, if you will … Making the most with what they have, preconceived notions aren't even a concept or a thought … We, as people, are always wanting more and new and improved … The herd asks for hay, water, and pellets (as warranted). … That's it … OK, pasture time, yes … But nothing of the physical and material world that we have polluted our dreams and aspirations with … None of the newest electronic gizmos, the newest cars, the newest fad, anything and everything MATERIAL that will make our lives easier and better … Family notwithstanding, I have found that the ONLY thing that has made MY existence and MY life easier and better, is the presence of the alpacas and dogs and others within the 4 fences of our farm … I find it infinitely easier to navigate through a hungry herd of alpacas, then to try and make my way through the holiday crowd at any one of a million malls in this great country … Alpacas and others will make way for you to feed them and then keep an eye on you as you give them their daily sustenance … Even when we are on the road with a small part of the herd for the shows that we attend, something quite remarkable invariably happens ... If we are stalling with another farm, our kids and theirs, will coexist, mostly harmoniously, in the equivalent of a studio apartment ... For 3-4 days, with members of a strange and different herd, and at the end of the show, surprisingly, everyone is ok ... There were no deadly shootings, no felonious assaults, no blood shed of any kind. ... Just, "hey, ok, see you at MOPACA" ... If we, as human beings, could be that secure, that accommodating to others within the human herd, think of all of the things we could actually LEARN from one another ... the memories we could create and the ideas that could be shared ... we try so hard, as a species, to tear down and obliterate the things we don't understand, and try to control and command the ones we think are inferior to us ... I believe that all living things on this planet have things to teach to us, things that we could use and value in our daily dealings with each other ... Will there be differences..? Of course, but if we are able to be civil and discuss things calmly and knowledgeably, we could learn so much, without compromising ourselves and, perhaps, making a few more friends along the way ...

Sacred Wavelength Remastered ...

The solace and quiet care from the animals, domesticated and otherwise, has been an enormous godsend to all of us ... I am thoroughly convinced that they see us and feel us as one of "their own", if you will ... God has blessed us with every single one of them ...

The last 6 months of my life has given me a completely new, ever deepening, increasingly enlightened sense and feeling of connection ... of being in tune, whether "full on" or little by little bits here and there.. How we are able to have THAT ... across borders, across cultures and languages and even SPECIES ... Levels of eye contact, little amounts of mutual trust and respect and acknowledgement of existence ... The same is true with the negative: averted gaze, distrust, and preconceived ideas about this other being, without being willing to explore and learn further, that connection is cut ... This is where fear and hate come from ...

Mismanaged personal educational opportunities ...

Giving yourself a chance to share even a moment with a soul, human or otherwise, and open the possibility of a connection ... to be in the moment, be with the moment, one ...

The ones I say a prayer for, the ones that have said prayers for me, for us. ... The ones that I respect for their resiliency in the face of obstacle, the beautiful ones we have never met, or only briefly on one of the stops on our journey, who have dropped everything just to say hi ... The ones who enlighten my existence simply by their existence ... The ones whose connection is still as strong today, as the day their spirits were set free, incorporating that connection and wavelength into the world ... The ones who have guided me in everything I know, everything I believe, everything I am ...

These are the connections that keep my mind in check, my heart in place, and my soul a little more upright ...

Namaste ...

Connectivity ...

On one level or another, we are all connected ... Either through blood or choice or circumstance or fate ... You connect with someone whether they know it or not, with a thought ... All of the people and beings in our lives get that fleeting thought and the spark is the connection ... that "feeling" when someone who has passed, is seeing things through your eyes, both for the first time ... sitting in our "courtyard" at Casa de mi Abuela in Arequipa with my wife, Rael, and a few birds, nothing to do, nowhere to go, and enjoying the "us" time. ... The bumpy roads in the Highlands. holding hands in the van, as we watch the beauty of of the countryside unfurl before our eyes, every mile marker, a vista; every road sign, an invitation ... The majesty of the Catholic faith in Peru, reconnected me with my grandmother, a wonderful Catholic woman from Woonsocket, Rhode

Island, who, basically taught my mother and I about truly, TRULY being a good Catholic … Old school …

The one night we stayed in Coporaque, we had the joy and the honor of watching the sunset over the valley, putting a blanket of night over the landscape for the earth to sleep, and wake up the next morning to the vast expanse of land before us, renewed and baptized in light, with Peruvian early spring color awash in the entire valley … That night at Chelawasi with friends, and friends to be, connecting over James Brown and Ginger beer … The people we met, within our group and the people of Peru, created a memory for all of us, and established that connection … Be it in person, face to Facebook, email, MAIL mail, or other correspondence, we connect, and in that, we learn, we grow into the person that we are destined to become …

Being able to connect with the animals as well, here and there, has a very important purpose in my life … Why..? Innocence and simplicity. … Doing all for the good of the tribe, the pack, the herd … The primal One, being a part of the Earth and the living system within … So many trying to tear the global herd apart, when we should take the example of our "uncivilized, uncultured" 4 legged friends around us and focus on the good, and work together for the good of the many …

Respect existence or expect resistance …

We are all connected …

Chaku …

A celebration..

A meditation …

A way of life for the community around Picotani …

The blessing of the harvest of the year; the fleece of the 2500 vicuna that roam this region ... 40,000+ acres where they live, protected and revered for what they provide this community, this country ...

Morning broke, and we were ready to observe one of the most fascinating and blessed rituals in all of Peru ... We made our way to Picotani, a very small, very primitive town in the highlands ... High plains, with magnificent vistas, and vicuna everywhere ... we grew more and more excited about what we were about to witness..

We arrived and the whole town and the whole community was on hand; many having never seen gringos before ... As it turns out, they didn't have enough people on hand to fully "staff" the round up, so our group was asked to participate ...

... to participate ...

We were told afterward that this was the first time that these people of the remote highlands had ever, EVER let gringos out into the fields where the vicuna run ...

We had the ceremony opening the day for the community and us ... One praying, blessing, gathering and helping, all for the greater good ... Thanking the Creator for all of the people gathered, the ones who could not attend, and the ones who came before them ... Ancestors who have done it this way for centuries ... The blessing was done, and the celebration and work of the day began ... as did the hail. ... We took the van out where the rocks began, and the hail made it impossible for the vans to continue across the rough terrain, and as the hail subsided, we exited and walked to where we would do our part to help ... Sitting among the rocks, finding bits of bone here and there ... The women of the community looking at us, not sure what to think ...

The head herdsmen of the community rode ahead of all us to the outer parts of the reserve to move the animals toward us, and toward the harvest of Picotani gold ... Representatives of the Government of Peru were also on hand to make sure that these animals were being treated in the manner of royalty, as was Carlos, a gentleman who is the areas most renowned expert on ALL things vicuna; a shaman, if you will ... He led the blessings and the chaku ...

As we waited, we started to see single and double random vicuna come into the lower valley ... Then, like magic, they crested the top of the hill, 150 acres away. ... More and more with every passing second coming over the hill, to us ... Village women and young adults flanked left and right, with us in the middle, among the boulders ... Three, then five.. ... Fifteen.. Thirty ... They kept coming. ... Down to the lower valley where they would be funneled into a tremendous catch pen ...

The last ones came through the rocks and both ends of the human chain were closed; a single line of humanity, stretching as far as the eye could see ... One purpose, one goal ... the betterment of the community.. Walking shoulder to shoulder with the people of this community, assisting in their harvest, their gold ... Nothing was said, only looks and smiles. ... And understanding ... .without a word ...

Closing in and funneling 2500 vicunas is a difficult proposition, and as the entire herd started to calm, the elder vicunas taking "charge" and re-assuring the young that they will be alright ...

The gate was closed and the celebration began. ...

Carlos, our leader, and host, leading the community in giving thanks to the Creator for their success ... Thanks to all in the community ... Thanks to our group, The Quechua Benefit, for our assistance and willingness to comply to all of their laws and traditions ... Thanks to the ancestors for their guidance.. And thanks to PachaMamma (Mother Earth), for all they have ...

Traditional dance and music, and blessings ...

As we were leaving, both Carlos and Moises, our host at the Mallkini Ranch, came up to me and, as neither spoke English, extended their hands and a smile; a genuine smile of friendship and brotherhood ... I shook their hands and hugged both, thanking them for this opportunity, and this blessing ...

A little boy walked up as we were getting in the van and stuck out his hand to me. ... Thanks, meester. ... The smile on his face, a mile wide ...

Thanksgiving. ... Becoming a part of something larger than yourself, for the common good ... Witnessing that, being a part of that ...

A moment ... a glorious moment ...

Chaku..

Colors ...

The ones we see with our eyes, the ones we see with our heart, our mind ... even our soul, I think ... In the course of an average week, we see so many shades of so many shades that our minds are kind of numb to it.. Living in a neighborhood, you see so many pastel, somewhat artificial, colors in the dwellings and decor ... Outside of the average production neighborhood, here in the country, the colors here are more natural, more vibrant, more "real" to the eye ... The wide open spaces in the Spring at sunset ... A partly cloudy February morning, 3 minutes before sunrise ... The back pasture the morning after a large snowfall ... the blues within the snow and ice that cover the landscape, untouched, pure, almost sacred ... The colors of red, orange and purple that emanate from the horizon when the day is set to begin, and again when the day is put to rest ... These are the colors that speak to me, to my soul ... Every once in a while, I am fortunate enough to be able to capture some of what I see, and try to convey the absolute beauty and sanctity that I experience, here on our farm ... I can only hope that the ones who see these can be moved to experience the same ... So many different shades of different shades here ... the ones that purify the mind and heart from a very natural place ... The ones that have touched my soul and my consciousness ...

I find, more and more lately, that I am most "myself" here ... 5 acres that have become a safe haven from the congested chaos of the city and "civilization" ... We came out to the country to get AWAY from civilization ... We already have to spend a great deal of our time in the city in our day jobs, and we experience all manner of everyone's "laundry", dirty and otherwise.. Sometimes it can get so monotonous and negative, that at the end of a day like that, I really need dose of "here" ...

The peace and solitude of the farm, and the quiet of open spaces in the evening while watching the crias run and jump and play, is the decompression mechanism that evens everything out ... Having the opportunity, even now that the days start to shorten, of spending even 20 minutes in the pens and just be with them, unimpeded and trusted, for the most part ... It has a wonderful way of changing the entire mindset after a day in civilization ...

Scars ...

They remind us of a situation, a time in our lives, a moment of hardship, of fear, of sorrow ... We try to cover them up; with long sleeves, jeans, shoes, hats ... I look in the mirror each morning, and in the harsh light above the sink, they are there, reminding me each day of my life. Like bookmarks or a highlighter, they are there. I see 52 years of moments, etched as in a statue. I see the good times, I see the bad. And each one, while it has a story attached, also has a lesson that comes with it.

The ones that are easier to cover up, at least for me, are the ones behind my eyes; the ones that no one else sees. Some of the demons that reside there are easier to cage than others, but as in the physical scars, these also have lessons attached. And at any given time, the inside scars present a new lesson, a new light, a new way to deal with the life that we have been presented.

As a society, we are conditioned to believe that scars are ugly; imperfections that detract from the beauty of a life. I disagree. I believe that they are proof of a life. We have scars as a reminder of this life and all of the events, happenstances, moments and beings that have inhabited and happened to us within this journey. Badges of honor to remind us that, this will not kill me. I will learn, grow and survive in spite and because of them. I will become the better, truer version of myself.

That is where the beauty resides. True beauty is in the life we have and the lessons that help us grow and become the best version of ourselves ...

Rhythm ...

If you listen, in the hard cold of winter, in the high plains of Colorado, you can hear it. The heartbeat ... It is so faint, it is almost unintelligible. But it's there ... Something I didn't even realize until we moved to the country.. In the city every season has it's hum and drone, drowning out even the smallest sounds and rhythms within the planet. At every time, day or night. Even here in the spring, summer and fall, there are the sounds of the insects, and the noises of the outside animals they make that contribute to the beats of life on the planet.

But the winter ...

3 am on a January or February morning, just before the crescent moon rises. 12 degrees outside without the wind blowing. It is still. Quiet. Peaceful and contemplative. A thin layer of snow rests on the ground, and the inhabitants of the house, the farm, the community, slumber.

A chance. A chance to walk outside and go into the front yard, and con-nect, as no other time in the year. The cold is secondary to the tranquility and peacefulness of the moments. I clear my mind and my soul, and listen. Just listen. Here is where absolute quiet and stillness lay. After I am clear, I hear it; I feel it.

Stillness in motion ... the slightest of sounds surround me for a second, then nothing. Again ... Then again ... and again ... then silence ...

I close my eyes and hear the snow start to fall, long before I feel the crystalline forms touch my skin. A sound so unique, it is impossible to describe; all I know is that this is the sound of heaven. The sound of an angels wings …

Stillness in motion …

The possible …

Even in the face of mental, spiritual and physical obstacles that everyday life tends to throw in the way, I remain standing.

Defiantly optimistic about the future, pushing ever forward, no matter what gets in the way. In days past, I would let the negative fester and permeate my entire being; my entire everything.

Not anymore …

There is so much to positively look forward to, to let a few bad apples ruin it for my being. Those who put their agendas in the way will be dismissed and treated with extreme indifference. I will fight for my happiness, contentment and peace, but not with physical violence. I will fight with example and a solid resolve to make my point of passion clear.

Crystal clear.

I will use my words as an educational weapon, so as to render those who oppose, defenseless and knocked senseless by the resolve of my soul and my being. I will fight the good fight, for those who can't fight. I will not lower myself to those who choose to use tactics contrary to my end game.

Purposely passionate about a passionate purpose.

Peace and tranquility.

One love. For all.

OF the people, FOR the people, BY the people …

I will NEVER be a politician. They cause so many of the problems facing our great country today. A bunch of rich guys in suits, making laws that really don't make sense, telling ALL of us how we should live our lives. I thought that we were the land of the free. I KNOW we are the home of the brave … They remind me of car salesmen, trying to get 40,000 dollars for a car that isn't worth 7500.00 … They promise this and promise that to get the votes they need to get into office, only to abandon their promises and create their own agenda … To the highest bidder, of course. … It really doesn't matter if you are a Democrat or a Republican or even a Tea Party member … It's all politics and the top 2% of the people with the most money are the ones that really win … Not us; the 98% who claw and scratch every day just to make ends meet … We, the 98%, are the ones that make this country what it is today; products and services that keep the country in the black. We, the 98%, are the ones making sacrifices so our animals and our families are fed, housed and kept warm on these cold autumn nights.. We, the 98%, are the ones busting our asses to make and keep a future for the ones who will come after us, making sure that things are run right … We should stand as ONE great nation, but we are divided over loyalties to our respective political parties; Democrat / Republican / Tea Party / whatever … We should stand as one, but we are divided by sexual preferences / religious beliefs / socio-economic status / personal beliefs, etc … Judgment abounds on those who are different in their thoughts, words and actions, and that's wrong … I believe that, no matter who you are, your strength of character is what makes you, you.. Not all the other crap … If you believe in God, or don't believe in God, fine … That's you.. If you are white or brown or black, that's fine … That's you … Every individual in this country has a right to believe in what they believe; as long as it doesn't hurt anyone in the process … I have had moments where I have judged people by the color of their skin, by their political affiliation, by their religious preferences, and, well, I was wrong … I can admit my own errors in judgment … I can now see the forest for the trees. People can change if they REALLY WANT TO.. Getting older, at least for me, has meant becoming wiser, and realizing that there is a lesson in absolutely everything … EVERYTHING …

I believe that we should have affordable medical care for our families and our animals, I believe that the people should decide, not the politicians. I believe that everyone has a right to 3 meals a day and a warm place to call home. I believe that anyone who abuses an animal should face the same abuse themselves and be tried as someone who abuses or kills another human being. I believe that we should all just look at each other as equals, and not as a competitor or an adversary.. I can and will talk to everybody, and if anything I have said here offends you; GOOD … It means you're paying attention … If you want to make the world a better place, take a look at yourself and make that change … Of the people, for the people, BY THE PEOPLE, One herd, under Canada, above Mexico, indivisible, with Liberty and justice for ALL …

Merry Christmahanakwazaakah …

This year has brought many highs and lows, and for all of these we are grateful. We have learned from all of these experiences, both good and bad and we continue to grow and move forward with the valuable lessons that all of these experiences give us.

I am grateful to my family and my family of friends. You are all extremely important to my growth as a husband, as a father, as an uncle, and as a human being. Thank you all for being in my life. My entire experience would not be complete without each and every one of you. Thank you to the ones that have come before us and left their mark with words and experiences that have molded me and us into the people we are today, specifically Margaret Anne Reddick [Mom], Rebecca Waesche [Mom also], Harry Lee Waesche [Grampi] and Virginia Waesche [Gramma Teeter] … Also in my thoughts and experiences this holiday season are both of my grandparents [Gramma and Grandpa Taylor] who left us long ago, but are never really far away. I am who I am because of all of you.

A most Merry Christmas to all and may the peace and tranquility of the season envelope you and keep you safe, happy and warm for now and the rest of your lives.

Peace on Earth and good will to all.

Tis the Season ...

It's beginning to look a lot like Christmas ... Everywhere you go ... In this time of giving, we believe its important to remember why we have the season in the first place.. Loving and caring, helping and sharing, trying to show all of those close to us that they matter and that we care about them and what happens in their lives ... We also believe that its important to show these values to those who are not as fortunate as us; those who don't have close family around them, those who are not as happy during this holiday season ... Tell someone you care and mean it ... Hug someone just because ... Send a card or a letter to someone you normally wouldn't ... Make a positive difference in someone's day ... And not just at Christmas.. Make the effort all year long, and it will start to spread ... We watch all year long as pain and heartache spread like wildfire throughout our communities and our nation ... So much hate and acrimony lately that it is making a difference; a negative difference.. We believe that the same thing can happen with hope and positivity ... If you take the positive and spread it, it will grow as well.. Embrace the differences between us; that's why we are all INDIVIDUALS ... You don't always have to agree with someone, but it's important to respect their point of view ... You don't always have to like someone, but respect their existence ... Become part of a bigger, better herd ... Why..? Just because ... That's why ... Peace on Earth and good will towards men ...

I watch ...

I see ...

I observe ...

I hear ...

I listen …

… and I learn.

I learn about such things as anger, jealousy, rage, reaction, contempt, and hatred.

I am also learning a great deal about love, about unity, about hope …

I see people who are willing to go the extra mile to help people; people who they have never met, to see that they are treated fairly, with respect and honor.

I also see people reacting on social media, to friends they have had for a very long time, in such a way as to villianize these "friends" for their opinion, and proceed to call them names, curse at them, and belittle them on a social platform, to prove their platform. I have seen reactions of a hostile, violent nature towards opinions and the actions of others. I have seen responses that are peaceful in nature to those who are being persecuted for what they believe, and how they choose to pray.

The only thing certain, in this time, is uncertainty. There are those who seek to divide us into groups, and conquer us all by doing so. I have seen the fear, I have seen the desperation. But I have also seen hope and love …

… and I pray …

I pray that the non-violent collective consciousness and positive energy of the planet can overcome, overrun and defeat those who wish to see us defeated. I pray that we, the people can rise above the acrimony and discord, to show the ones who bait; the ones who hate, that the power of love, respect and honor will always be the better way …

Indivisible …

As I roll out of bed every morning, I am grateful.

Grateful for the opportunity to be able to get out of bed and live another day on this planet.

Grateful for the family that is still here, and supports me in my endeavors.

Grateful for the family that has passed, for the continuing lessons and memories that teach me and enrich my life every single day.

Grateful for all of the people that we have in our lives that continually check on us, and include us in their lives, every day.

Grateful for the ones who decided that our situation was "far too difficult" to deal with and decided to step away. They know who they are.

Grateful for the family that did the same thing, as these lessons, while difficult, have proven to be the most telling of where we fit.

Grateful for the animals in our lives, as the "voice of reason", keeping us grounded in exactly what's important. For Thea and Isis, and the lessons these two magnificent cats have bestowed upon our being after the death of our son, their dad. For our canine companions who have shown us love, trust, protection and gratitude of their own. For the alpacas, whose lessons given, merely by being alive, were and continue to be, immeasurable.

Grateful for sunny days, and star filled nights to contemplate absolutely everything.

Grateful for the wind, that creates a myriad of momentary air sculptures, so beautiful to behold. For the snow, creating frozen sculptures, ever changing and evolving. For the rain, as it washes everything, and brings new life in the spring and summer. For the beauty of it all.

Grateful for music, and the peace, tranquility and meditation that it provides on a daily basis.

Grateful for the house we live in, and the beings, feelings and memories that make this a home.

Grateful for all of the places that I have been, the people I have encountered, and the experiences of both.

Grateful for people that I have never met in person, for sharing a part of themselves with me.

Grateful for the sunrise in Colorado, as the colors regenerate my spirit at the beginning of a new day.

Grateful for the sunset in St. Croix, as this provided a new and beautiful vantage point on this journey.

Grateful for the opportunities presented to me in this journey.

Grateful for each and every breath I have taken.

Grateful for every single experience I have had in my 50+ years of physical life.

Grateful for the lessons that have come, and all of the lessons-to-be.

Grateful to be able to be grateful.

ABOUT THE AUTHOR

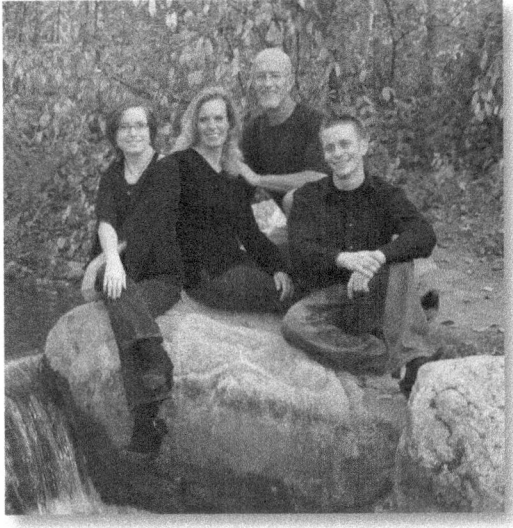

Born and raised in Aurora, Colorado, Danny never lived anymore than 30 minutes from his childhood home. That is until August 2018 when he and his wife of 25 years, took a leap of faith, and moved to the U.S. Virgin Islands, with their 4 dogs and their son's cat, aka Grandbaby. He is a proud husband and father, looking forward to next chapter of the journey.